A BUDGET FOR A

Better

America

PROMISES KEPT. TAXPAYERS FIRST

FISCAL YEAR 2020

BUDGET OF THE U.S. GOVERNMENT

THE BUDGET DOCUMENTS

Budget of the United States Government, Fiscal Year 2020 contains the Budget Message of the President, information on the President's priorities, and summary tables.

Analytical Perspectives, Budget of the United States Government, Fiscal Year 2020 contains analyses that are designed to highlight specified subject areas or provide other significant presentations of budget data that place the budget in perspective. This volume includes economic and accounting analyses; information on Federal receipts and collections; analyses of Federal spending; information on Federal borrowing and debt; baseline or current services estimates; and other technical presentations.

Supplemental tables and other materials that are part of the *Analytical Perspectives* volume are available at *https://www.whitehouse.gov/omb/analytical-perspectives/*.

Appendix, Budget of the United States Government, Fiscal Year 2020 contains detailed information on the various appropriations and funds that constitute the budget and is designed primarily for the use of the Appropriations Committees. The *Appendix* contains more detailed financial information on individual programs and appropriation accounts than any of the other budget documents. It includes for each agency: the proposed text of appropriations language; budget schedules for each account; legislative proposals; narrative explanations of each budget account; and proposed general provisions applicable to the appropriations of entire agencies or group of agencies. Information is also provided on certain activities whose transactions are not part of the budget totals.

Major Savings and Reforms, Fiscal Year 2020, which accompanies the President's Budget, contains detailed information on major savings and reform proposals. The volume describes both major discretionary program eliminations and reductions and mandatory savings proposals.

GENERAL NOTES

1. All years referenced for budget data are fiscal years unless otherwise noted. All years referenced for economic data are calendar years unless otherwise noted.
2. At the time the Budget was prepared, five of the annual appropriations bills for 2019 had been enacted (the Energy and Water Development and Related Agencies Appropriations Act, 2019; the Legislative Branch Appropriations Act, 2019; the Military Construction, Veterans Affairs, and Related Agencies Appropriations Act, 2019; the Department of Defense Appropriations Act, 2019; and the Departments of Labor, Health and Human Services, and Education, and Related Agencies Appropriations Act, 2019). The programs and activities provided for in the seven remaining 2019 annual appropriations bills were operating under a continuing resolution (Public Law 115-245, as amended). For these programs, references to 2019 spending in the text and tables reflect the levels provided by the continuing resolution (except for the *Major Savings and Reforms* (MSV) volume which was written following enactment of all appropriations and reflects 2019 enacted for all programs).
3. Detail in this document may not add to the totals due to rounding.

ISBN: 978-1-64143-357-0

Table of Contents

Page

The Budget Message of the President 1
A Budget for a Better America 5
Modernizing Government 7
Cutting the Red Tape: Unleashing Economic Freedom 13
Department of Agriculture 15
Department of Commerce 19
Department of Defense 23
Department of Education 29
Department of Energy 35
Department of Health and Human Services 39
Department of Homeland Security 49
Department of Housing and Urban Development 53
Department of the Interior 57
Department of Justice 61
Department of Labor 65
Department of State and Other International Programs 71
Department of Transportation 77
Department of the Treasury 81
Department of Veterans Affairs 85
Corps of Engineers—Civil Works 89
Environmental Protection Agency 93
National Aeronautics and Space Administration 97
Small Business Administration 101
Summary Tables 105
OMB Contributors to the 2020 Budget 141

THE BUDGET MESSAGE OF THE PRESIDENT

To the Congress of the United States:

In just over 2 years, together with the American people, we have launched an unprecedented economic boom. Since I was elected, we have created more than 5 million new jobs, including half a million manufacturing jobs. Nearly 5 million Americans have been lifted off food stamps. Unemployment is the lowest in nearly half a century. African American unemployment, Hispanic American unemployment, and Asian American unemployment rates have all reached historic lows. Our Nation is experiencing an economic miracle—and it is improving the lives of all our citizens.

We have achieved these extraordinary gains thanks to historic tax cuts and an unprecedented regulatory reduction campaign, through unleashing American energy production, systematically fixing bad trade deals, and remaining absolutely committed to putting the needs of the American worker first.

My Administration worked with the Congress to pass unprecedented legislation to confront the opioid crisis, a sweeping new farm bill, groundbreaking criminal justice reform, major investments to rebuild the military, and historic Department of Veterans Affairs reforms to ensure that our great veterans have access to high quality healthcare.

We are also making our communities safer. To target violent crime, my Administration has increased support for Federal, State, and local law enforcement. We have added nearly 200 new violent crime prosecutors across the United States. And last year, the Department of Justice prosecuted more violent crimes than ever before. As a result, violent crime is falling.

My Administration is confronting the national security and humanitarian crisis on our southern border, and we are accepting the moral duty to create an immigration system that protects the lives and jobs of our citizens. This includes our obligation to the millions of immigrants living in the United States today who followed the rules and respected our laws.

In the 20th century, America saved freedom, transformed science, and defined the middle class standard of living. Now we must write the next chapter of the great American adventure, turbocharging the industries of the future and establishing a new standard of living for the 21st century. An amazing quality of life for all of our citizens is within reach. We can make our communities safer, our families stronger, our culture richer, our faith deeper, and our middle class bigger and more prosperous than ever before.

We are now addressing our challenges from a position of strength. My 2020 Budget builds on the tremendous progress we have made and provides a clear roadmap for the Congress to bring Federal spending and debt under control. We must protect future generations from Washington's habitual deficit spending.

This year, I asked most executive departments and agencies to cut their budgets by at least 5 percent. In addition to reflecting those reductions, my Budget invests in the following priorities:

Securing our Borders and Protecting our Sovereignty. As President, my highest duty is the defense of our Nation—which is why finishing the border wall is an urgent national priority. All who are privileged to hold elected office must work together to create an immigration system that promotes wage growth and economic opportunity, while preventing drugs, terrorism, and crime from entering the United States. Immigration policy, like all policy, must serve the interests of Americans living here today—including the millions of new Americans who came here legally to join our national family. The American people are entitled to a strong border that stops illegal immigration, and a responsible visa policy that protects our security and our workforce. My Budget continues to reflect these priorities, and I look forward to working with the Congress to finish the border wall and build a safe, just, and lawful immigration system that will benefit generations of Americans to come.

Preserving Peace through Strength. A strong military, fully integrated with our allies and all our instruments of power, enables our Nation to deter war, preserve peace, and, if necessary, defeat aggression against United States interests. To that end, my Budget requests $750 billion for national defense, an increase of $34 billion, or 5 percent, from the 2019 enacted level. The Budget funds the National Security Strategy and National Defense Strategy, building on the major gains we have already made throughout the world.

Protecting our Veterans. Our Nation's brave warriors and defenders deserve the best care America has to offer—both during and after their active service. Last year, I signed into law the historic VA MISSION Act of 2018 to reform and transform the Department of Veterans Affairs healthcare system into an integrated system for the 21st century. My Budget fully funds all requirements for veterans' healthcare services and provides additional funding to implement the VA MISSION Act of 2018.

Investing in America's Students and Workers. To help protect taxpayer dollars, my Budget continues my request to create an educational finance system that requires postsecondary institutions that accept taxpayer funds to have skin in the game through a student loan risk-sharing program. My Administration will also continue to seek expanded Pell Grant eligibility for high-quality, short-term programs in high-demand fields, so that students and workers can quickly gain valuable skills at a more affordable cost and obtain family-sustaining jobs. We must create and invest in better opportunities for our Nation's students and job seekers, while ensuring that we do so in a more efficient and effective manner.

Research for Childhood Cancers. Many childhood cancers have not seen new therapies in decades. My Budget initiates a new effort that invests $500 million over the next 10 years to support this critical life-saving research.

Defeating HIV/AIDS in America. The HIV epidemic still plagues our Nation, with more than 38,000 Americans infected every year. In response, my Budget provides $291 million to the Department of Health and Human Services to defeat the HIV/AIDS epidemic. The goal is to eliminate most new infections within 5 years (75 percent) and nearly all within 10 years (90 percent). This initiative will focus efforts on diagnosis, prevention, and treatment efforts in the locations where intense transmissions of the virus are driving the epidemic.

Confronting the Opioid Epidemic. My Budget continues historic levels of funding for our law enforcement, prevention, and treatment efforts to combat the opioid and drug addiction epidemic.

Supporting Working Families. America must also lead in supporting the families of our workforce so that they can balance the competing demands of work and family. My Budget includes a one-time, mandatory investment of $1 billion for a competitive fund aimed at supporting underserved populations and stimulating employer investments in child care for working families. My Administration has also pledged to provide paid parental leave to help working parents, and we are committed to partnering with the Congress to enact this important policy.

******

We must always strive to uphold our oaths to promote and protect the personal and economic freedoms the Constitution guarantees to us all.

We must work together to renew the bonds of love and loyalty that link us to one another—as friends, as citizens, as neighbors, as patriots, and as Americans.

My Budget reflects my Administration's commitment to these worthy goals as it seeks to make the United States of America wealthier, stronger, safer, and greater for every American family and neighborhood.

DONALD J. TRUMP

THE WHITE HOUSE,
MARCH 11, 2019

A BUDGET FOR A BETTER AMERICA

Over the past two years, the President has restored faith in the American dream and extended a more prosperous future—an American future—that is secure, sovereign, and affordable.

The President's pro-growth economic agenda, MAGAnomics, has unleashed the American economy. Working alongside Republicans in the Congress, the President signed historic tax reform into law, marking the first time in more than 30 years that the Nation's tax laws were overhauled to provide much-needed relief to American Families, all while allowing U.S. small businesses to flourish. Unemployment is the lowest in 50 years, millions of jobs have been created, and GDP grew by 3.1 percent over the four quarters of 2018. For the first time in history, there are more vacant jobs than job seekers to fill them. The economic health of the Nation is as strong as it has ever been.

The Administration's ongoing efforts to cut red tape are also key to continued economic growth. Over the past year, Federal agencies have eliminated 12 unnecessary or duplicative regulations for every one new regulation implemented, which has saved the economy more than $23 billion in Washington-imposed costs. The President's deregulatory efforts are providing relief for all Americans through real wage growth and more jobs, ushering in a new era of optimism. The weight of Washington's presence is now a more distant memory, and Americans feel confident to invest in their families, businesses, and future.

However, for economic growth to endure, Washington must fix its longtime spending problem, which has driven the Nation's debt to more than $22 trillion this year. Even with high levels of economic growth, excessive deficits continue to threaten the Nation's progress, and any unforeseen shocks to the economy could make deficits unsustainable. Without action to restore the proper size and role of the Government, deficits will remain over a trillion dollars per year for the foreseeable future. Debt, already run up by the excesses of previous administrations' economic policies, will soon surpass a percent of GDP not seen since 1947.

If financial obligations continue to grow at the current pace, the Nation's creditors may demand higher interest rates to compensate, potentially leading to lower private investment and a smaller capital stock, harming both American businesses and workers. If nothing is done, interest payments alone on the Federal Government's debt will double by 2023 and exceed spending on the U.S. military by 2024.

Even with a booming economy, excluding Social Security and Medicare spending and revenues, the Federal Government is still running a net deficit of $608 billion. During the Great Recession, this figure increased from $664 billion in 2008 to $1,354 billion in 2010, illustrating what can happen during changes in the business cycle when there is a complete lack of fiscal restraint. Since the end of the recession, little has been done to rein in excessive spending as net deficits averaged $759 billion from 2010–2016.

The President is committed to protecting and respecting American taxpayers. Recognizing the importance of controlling excessive spending, the President directed Federal agencies to reduce their programmatic spending to five percent below the non-Defense discretionary budget cap. Only in Washington would that be considered impossible. Ordinary, hard-working American families make necessary sacrifices daily to provide for their families. Washington should be no different.

Yet, facing up to fiscal reality does not mean ignoring the other needs facing the Nation. The Budget demonstrates how, even within this constrained discretionary topline, the President proposes to fund critical national priorities by reprioritizing other spending. The Budget protects or increases funding for border security, national defense, opioids, law enforcement, childcare, veterans' healthcare, emerging technologies that support the industries of the future, and workforce development. The Budget also illustrates the Administration's commitment to rebuilding the Nation's infrastructure and addressing high drug prices.

The 2020 Budget builds off the foundation of the President's previous budgets and provides an avenue toward spending restraint. The Budget meets the President's directive on spending reductions by agency, proposing over $2.7 trillion in spending reductions—more proposed spending reductions than any previous administration in history—and closing out the 10-year budget window with spending below the post-war average of 20 percent of GDP. Once again, with the Budget, the President provides his vision to get the Nation's fiscal house back in order to provide a better America for you.

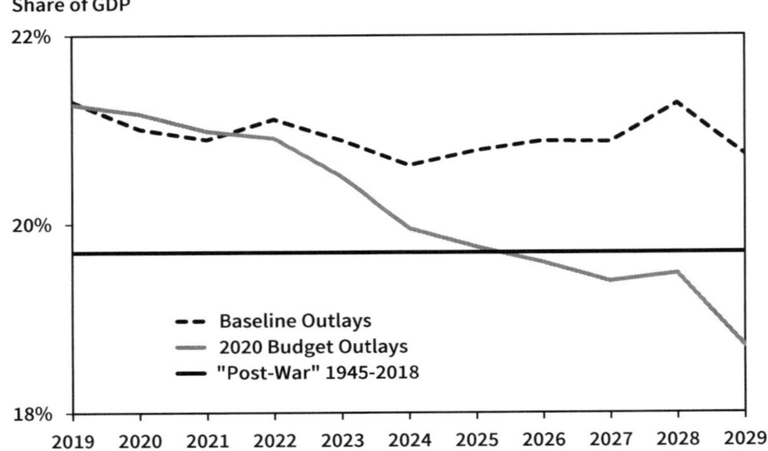

MODERNIZING GOVERNMENT

The 2020 Budget supports the Administration's work to modernize Government for the 21st Century. The American people deserve a modern Government that will refocus efforts on core mission areas, provide excellent customer service, and ensure accountable stewardship.

The President's Management Agenda (PMA) lays the foundation for a portfolio of work to address critical challenges where Government has failed to keep up with technical advances and business process improvements.

PRESIDENT'S MANAGEMENT AGENDA

The PMA outlines a long-term vision for an effective Government that better achieves its missions and enhances key services on which the American people depend. It advances three drivers of change—technology, data, and the workforce—through multiple paths, recognizing that real transformation requires cross-functional change across disciplines. The PMA sets 14 Cross-Agency Priority (CAP) Goals where Executive Branch agencies can collaborate to drive modernization, including critical areas such as cybersecurity, customer experience, payment accuracy, information technology (IT), human resources, and procurement.

IT Modernization

The 2020 Budget supports agency investments to modernize IT systems and improve the value they provide to the American people.

Modernizing Government Technology (MGT) Provisions[1] and the Technology Modernization Fund (TMF). MGT provisions provide financial resources and technical expertise to improve Federal technology. A key component of the MGT provisions is the TMF, which enables agencies to reimagine and transform how technology is used to deliver mission and services. Agencies propose projects to a TMF Board and, if selected and funded, repay funds within five years.

- From among nearly 50 proposals totaling over $500 million in the first 10 months, the Board has so far funded seven projects totaling almost $90 million. Projects are listed at *https://tmf.cio.gov.*
- The Administration requests $150 million for the TMF in 2020 to provide seed funding for additional projects and to allow the TMF to tackle more complex, Government-wide efforts.

In addition, MGT provisions authorized agencies to establish IT Working Capital Funds (WCFs) as a dedicated resource for IT modernization. The Budget requests necessary transfer authority to better enable agencies to operationalize these IT WCFs and fully implement flexibilities of the MGT provisions. The Budget reflects instances where agencies are establishing IT WCFs.

Modernizing IT to Increase Productivity and Security (CAP Goal 1). Through this goal, the Administration is building and maintaining more modern, secure, and resilient IT to enhance mission delivery and productivity.

- Federal Agencies have delivered on the action items provided in the *Report to the President on Federal IT Modernization*,

[1] Pub. L. No. 115-91, National Defense Authorization Act for Fiscal Year 2018, Title X, Subtitle G (§§ 1076 through 1078).

completing all of the 52 tasks outlined and informing further priorities and next steps included in this goal.

- The Administration released Office of Management and Budget (OMB) Memorandum M-19-03, Strengthening the Cybersecurity of Federal Agencies by enhancing the High Value Asset Program, creating a formal program to support all agencies in High Value Asset identification, assessment, remediation, and response to incidents.
- The Administration released the draft *2018 Federal Cloud Computing Strategy* on September 24, 2018, for public comment, soliciting feedback from industry, agencies, and the American people.
- The Administration released a draft memorandum, Strengthening the Cybersecurity of Federal Agencies through Improved Identity, Credential, and Access Management, on April 6, 2018, for public comment, to better control information access and protect information.
- The Department of Homeland Security (DHS) and OMB piloted enhancements to the cybersecurity controls required by the Trusted Internet Connection program.
- Agencies continue to implement the Continuous Diagnostics and Monitoring program, with all Chief Financial Officers Act agencies now sharing data with the Federal Dashboard.

Data, Accountability, and Transparency

Leveraging Data as a Strategic Asset (CAP Goal 2). The Administration is creating the first comprehensive Federal Data Strategy for managing and using Federal data.

- In 2018, the Administration launched the Federal Data Strategy outlining Principles, Practices, and a Year 1 Action Plan on *https://strategy.data.gov*. The Data Incubator Project creates practical case studies for future complementary Federal data management and use.
- The Budget supports the Federal Data Strategy by establishing a U.S. Federal Data Service within the Department of Commerce's Office of the Undersecretary for Economic Affairs.
- The Administration will begin implementing the Foundations for Evidence-Based Policymaking Act of 2018, including designating agency Statistical Officials and Chief Data Officers, requiring machine-readable data, improving secure access to data, and strengthening privacy protections.
- The Budget supports the Federal Geographic Data Committee's work to improve management of geospatial data and implement the provisions of the Geospatial Data Act of 2018.

Workforce for the 21st Century

Developing a Workforce for the 21st Century (CAP Goal 3). The Federal workforce represents a critical part of realizing change. Failure to address fundamental workforce needs will render other modernization work ineffective. This goal reflects a transformational shift in strategic human capital management based on three pillars:

1. Actively Managing the Workforce: Improving employee performance management and employee engagement;
2. Developing Agile Operations: Reskilling and redeploying human capital resources; and
3. Acquiring Top Talent: Enabling simple and strategic hiring practices.

The goal is co-led by OMB, the Office of Personnel Management (OPM), and the Department of Defense. DHS, the Departments of Veterans Affairs, Health and Human Services (HHS), and the Interior lead three subgoals. Almost all agencies participate in some capacity.

The first year of implementation focused on defining a baseline for how agencies address poor performers, distribute financial awards, and hire staff. The Administration is using existing authority to remove barriers and fix processes. Examples include issuing direct hire authority for science, technology, engineering, and mathematics positions; modernizing Senior Executive Service processes; strengthening performance management; and acting to increase employee engagement. Going forward, this goal will focus on continuous improvement within agencies.

Additional Focus Areas to Strengthen Mission, Service, and Stewardship

Improving Customer Experience (CAP Goal 4). Customer satisfaction with Federal services lags by as much as nine points behind the private sector. To close this gap, the Administration has identified Federal programs that provide the highest impact customer-facing services. These programs are implementing Government-wide customer feedback measures aligned with private-sector best practices and creating action plans for improvement. Performance data and action plans will be posted online for the public.

Agency Initiatives to Transform Customer Experience

The General Services Administration (GSA) and the U.S. Digital Service launched https://www.login.gov, a single, common identity platform that lets users access Government services more securely, easily, and quickly. This site has grown to more than 12 million users and continues to grow.

The Departments of Labor, Education, Defense, and Veterans Affairs; the Small Business Administration; GSA; and OPM have created an interagency journey map of how servicemembers interact with programs across Government during their transition to civilian employment. With this perspective, the team is now identifying improvements that matter most to the customer.

Sharing Quality Services (CAP Goal 5). This goal created a new shared service model to improve performance, customer experience, and operational costs. The new model establishes Government-wide centralized capabilities offered through Quality Service Management Offices that each oversee one functional area, such as financial management, procurement, payroll, etc. In an early effort to apply this model in 2018, GSA awarded blanket purchase agreements for the NewPay initiative for software as a service solutions for payroll and time and attendance services across Government. The Budget provides funds to begin migrating the Departments of Agriculture and the Interior and GSA to NewPay.

Shifting from Low-Value to High-Value Work (CAP Goal 6). The Administration has lifted nearly 60 redundant, obsolete, or unnecessary requirements from all Federal agencies and proposed to eliminate or modify more than 400 congressionally required plans and reports that are outdated or duplicative. In addition, OMB is coordinating with OPM and GSA to reform burdensome data collection and reporting requirements.

Category Management (CAP Goal 7). Increasing the use of proven, enterprise solutions for more than $300 billion in common goods and services allows the Government to leverage its buying power and reduce unnecessary, expensive duplication. As a result, the Government has avoided $17 billion in costs, applied category management principles to nearly 45 percent of common spend, exceeded metrics for use of top-tier Government-wide solutions by $11 billion, and exceeded small businesses goals.

Results-Oriented Accountability for Grants (CAP Goal 8). This goal helps maximize the value of grant funding by applying a risk-based, data-driven framework to balance compliance requirements with demonstrating successful results for the American taxpayer. The *Analytical Perspectives* chapter 17 "Aid to State and Local Governments" provides more information about this Goal.

Shifting to High-Value Work: Leveraging Technology

The Administration is using Robotics Process Automation and other emerging technologies to reduce error, improve compliance, and focus the Federal workforce on higher-value work.

GSA's Office of the Chief Financial Officer shifted staff to higher-value work after automating tasks that consumed approximately 12,000 labor hours per year at an estimated half the cost.

The National Aeronautics and Space Administration's Shared Services Center has four bots running nine different processes, including distributing funds, procurement, documenting images, scanning files, and creating folders to establish grants packages.

HHS is using artificial intelligence to help identify opportunities to consolidate contract vehicles, which will offer significant cost savings.

Getting Payments Right (CAP Goal 9). Preventing improper payments that result in a monetary loss is a high priority for the Administration. For additional details, please refer to the *Analytical Perspectives* volume chapter 9, "Payment Integrity," which includes Budget proposals aimed at preventing these improper payments.

Improving Outcomes through IT Cost Transparency (CAP Goal 10). This goal aims to leverage budget, acquisition, and financial data from authoritative sources using automation. Federal employees will be able to shift efforts to analysis and strategy recommendations rather than duplicating data entry, often not from authoritative sources.

Improving the Management of Major Acquisitions (CAP Goal 11). Federal agencies will ensure contracts supporting transformative and other priority projects will meet or beat delivery schedules, provide exceptional customer service, and achieve savings or cost avoidance for the taxpayer. The implementation strategy includes strengthening talent management and agency governance as well as tracking investments using portfolio management principles.

Modernizing Infrastructure Permitting (CAP Goal 12). The Administration is working to reduce the overall time to make decisions for major infrastructure projects with the goal of reducing time to an average of two years. These efforts have already resulted in $1 billion in cost savings through avoided permitting delays. The public can now track agency performance online at *https://www.permits.performance.gov*.

Security Clearance, Suitability, and Credentialing Reform (CAP Goal 13). This goal promotes a Federal workforce that reliably protects Federal Government people, property, systems, and information through an enhanced risk management framework.

Improving the Transfer of Federally Funded Technologies from Lab-to-Market (CAP Goal 14). This goal will strengthen the ability of federally funded innovations to transition from discovery in the laboratory to impact in the marketplace, including by reducing regulatory burden, strengthening partnerships, and enhancing how to measure return on Federal investment. See *Analytical Perspectives* chapter 21, "Research and Development," for more information.

OTHER PRIORITIES TO MODERNIZE GOVERNMENT

Government Reform and Reorganization. Another tool to modernize the Federal Government for today's mission needs is reorganization. In June 2018, the *Delivering Government Solutions in the 21st Century* plan laid out specific examples of organizational misalignment. The *Analytical Perspectives* volume chapter 8 provides more information about the Administration's reform priorities and phased implementation approach.

Acquisition Modernization. The Federal Government spends a half trillion dollars through contracts each year to help deliver the mission in hundreds of agencies. While user-driven and innovative acquisitions continue to achieve results, most agencies remain encumbered by an antiquated and complex system. The Administration will unveil an Acquisition Modernization Plan to guide incremental transformation through continuous process improvement testing, feedback, re-testing, and scaling. The Administration will work with the Congress on appropriate pilot authorities to allow tailored flexibility, if necessary, to test ideas to improve value and efficiency, consistent with principles of impartiality, transparency, and a robust supplier base.

Enterprise Risk Management (ERM). ERM is a tool to support strategic planning, improve performance, and foster a more risk-aware culture. In June 2018, OMB updated OMB Circular No. A-123, Appendix A, Management of Reporting and Data Integrity Risk, to integrate prior guidance for internal controls with current ERM policy. Agencies will now use a risk-based approach to assess, document, test, and report on internal controls over reporting and data integrity. Increasing maturity among agency ERM programs will support decision making across the PMA.

Performance Management. The Administration continues to leverage best practices from across sectors to drive improvement via the Federal Performance Management Framework. In 2018, agencies continued quarterly, data-driven performance reviews of over 80 Agency Priority Goals. OMB held strategic review meetings with the major agencies to discuss management successes, challenges, and risks for over 265 strategic objectives and identify course corrections where needed. The Administration also issued a five-year strategic plan with key strategies and guidance to implement the Program Management Improvement Accountability Act.

Strengthen Use of Evidence. To further implement the Foundations for Evidence-Based Policymaking Act of 2018, the Administration will direct agencies to establish multiyear learning agendas to strategically plan their evidence-building activities in order to improve policy and programs. Agencies will also designate an Evaluation Officer to help lead evidence-building activities.

Real Property. The Administration has prioritized optimizing the Federal real property portfolio to achieve the mission and minimize cost. The *Analytical Perspectives* volume chapter 10 describes recent accomplishments and the vision to achieve this reform.

CUTTING THE RED TAPE: UNLEASHING ECONOMIC FREEDOM

Since taking office, the President has reinvigorated the economy through an historic regulatory reform agenda. The American people can feel the effects of economic freedom as the Administration eliminates unduly burdensome regulations and pulls back the long reach of Federal mandates.

In 2018, the Administration removed 12 old regulations for every one new significant regulation and saved the American people $23 billion in overall regulatory costs. In just his first 21 months in office, the President achieved a total of $33 billion in net regulatory cost savings for the American people, a stark contrast to the $245 billion in net regulatory costs imposed by the Obama Administration during the same amount of time. The President's regulatory reform agenda represents a fundamental change of direction for the Federal Government. The strategy is simple: by eliminating or amending regulations that are duplicative, unnecessary, ineffective, or unduly burdensome, the Administration is unleashing the ingenuity, determination, and know-how of the private sector, which has always been the principal driver of American prosperity.

Comprehensive regulatory reform has provided relief to millions of Americans. The Department of Labor eased the burden on small business owners, affording them new opportunities to provide healthcare to their employees through association health plans. The Department of Veterans Affairs has expanded veterans' ability to use telecommunications to access healthcare providers, expanding options for those who live in rural and underserved areas. The Administration rolled back regulations on America's fishermen, providing a net economic benefit of over $654 million to that industry. The Department of Health and Human Services reduced healthcare paperwork burdens, saving $8.2 billion in regulatory costs and providing much-needed relief to Medicare providers. In a major report, the Council of Economic Advisers estimates that key Administration healthcare deregulatory actions that expanded choice of insurance coverage will produce massive economic benefit—on the magnitude of nearly $250 billion over a decade.

The Administration plans even bolder efforts during the remainder of 2019. Agencies plan deregulatory actions on Corporate Average Fuel Economy standards, Waters of the United States, and automated vehicles, resulting in even more benefits for the American people. While continuing to protect health and safety, the President's regulatory reform allows individuals and small businesses to produce and innovate. These bold actions will create jobs, spur innovation, and yield billions of dollars in benefits for American businesses and families.

Getting Washington out of the way promotes the American dream. The Administration's commonsense regulatory policy has renewed confidence in the economy so the American people can once again confidently invest in their families, businesses, and future.

DEPARTMENT OF AGRICULTURE

Funding Highlights:

- The U.S. Department of Agriculture (USDA) provides leadership and direction on issues related to food, agriculture, and natural resources based on sound public policy, the best available science, and effective management.
- The Budget focuses on core Departmental activities such as agricultural research, rural lending, and protecting the Nation's forested lands and private agricultural lands, while also supporting the Secretary's efforts to improve services and expand broadband. The Budget also proposes that USDA responsibly and efficiently use taxpayer resources by making targeted reforms to duplicative programs and overly generous subsidy programs.
- The 2020 Budget requests $20.8 billion for USDA, a $3.6 billion or 15-percent decrease from the 2019 estimate (including changes in mandatory programs and receipts).

The President's 2020 Budget:

USDA works to promote American agricultural products and exports, support rural economic development, maintain access to a safe and nutritious food supply, and strengthen the productive and sustainable use of National Forest System Lands and stewardship of private lands.

USDA's broad mission encompasses everything from domestic feeding programs and assistance in rural America, to farm loans and the National Forest System. Throughout rural America, USDA's programs provide financing to help grow job prospects and raise income levels as well as improve utilities and infrastructure. The Department works to promote agricultural production while also protecting the long-term availability of safe and affordable food. USDA programs safeguard and protect America's food supply by reducing the incidence of food-borne hazards through the inspection of meat, poultry, and egg products.

The Department's programs also improve nutrition and health through food assistance and nutrition education. USDA works to increase foreign market access for U.S. agricultural products and provides data and analysis of foreign market conditions. This helps U.S. agricultural producers make informed decisions on international trade opportunities, and supports the U.S. economy through increased exports. In addition, USDA manages and protects America's public and private lands by working cooperatively across Federal, State, and local governments and the private sector and the private sector to preserve and conserve the Nation's natural resources through restored forests, improved watersheds, and healthy private working lands. The Budget supports critical investments across core mission areas within USDA to best deliver results and support rural America.

Protects Health Outcomes for Pregnant Women, Infants, and Young Children. The Budget requests $5.8 billion to serve all projected participants in the Special Supplemental Nutrition Program for Women, Infants, and Children. This program provides nutritious supplemental food packages, nutrition education, and health and immunization referrals to low-income and nutritionally at-risk pregnant and postpartum women, infants, and children.

> *"[W]e will continue to provide the best possible service to our customers – the farmers, ranchers, foresters, and producers of American agriculture and 'do right and feed everyone'."*
>
> USDA Strategic Goals
> May 2018

Promotes Work and Reforms the Food Safety Net. The Budget includes bold proposals to help able-bodied adults participating in the Supplemental Nutrition Assistance Program (SNAP) enter the job market and work toward self-sufficiency. The Budget continues the America's Harvest Box proposal, allowing innovative partnerships with the private sector to combine the traditional SNAP Electronic Benefits Transfer benefits with 100 percent American grown foods provided directly to households. The proposal ensures that Americans in need have access to a nutritious diet while significantly reducing the cost to taxpayers. States maintain the ability to provide choice to their participants, including innovative approaches for the inclusion of fresh products. The Budget also includes proposals to reserve benefits for those most in need, promote efficiency in State operations, and strengthen program integrity.

Invests in Rural America. In today's information-driven global economy, e-connectivity has become an essential component to attract and grow rural businesses. To that end, the Budget supports continued implementation of the Secretary's e-Connectivity Pilot Program to foster thriving agricultural economies. The Department also helps to maintain and modernize rural utilities by providing critical support for infrastructure, such as $528 million in funding for water and wastewater grants and loans that support $1.2 billion in water and wastewater direct loans, $5.5 billion in electric loans, and $690 million in telecommunications loans. Through USDA's $24 billion portfolio of guaranteed housing loans, the Department assists lenders in providing low- to moderate-income rural Americans with access to affordable housing. In addition, the Budget supports a $3 billion loan level for community facility direct and guaranteed loans, which assist communities in developing or improving essential public services and facilities across rural America, such as health clinics or fire and rescue stations.

Combats the Opioid Challenge Facing Rural America. According to the Centers for Disease Control and Prevention, the rates of drug overdose deaths are rising in rural communities, surpassing the rate in urban areas. Through the Secretary's leadership of the Task Force on Agriculture and Rural Prosperity, the Department has identified specific actions to combat the opioid crisis and improve the quality of life in rural communities. USDA is approaching the opioid crisis with a dedicated urgency by partnering with local communities to provide program resources for prevention, treatment, and recovery. For example, USDA has launched an interactive data tool to help rural communities as they plan and build a local response to this monumental challenge. The Budget proposes $44 million in distance learning and telemedicine grants, of which $20 million would be dedicated to projects that combat the opioid crisis. In addition, the Budget proposes $60 million in community facilities grants, which can be used to support treatment centers and other community needs.

Prioritizes Agricultural Research. USDA funded research helps to protect, secure, and improve the Nation's food, agricultural, and natural resource systems. Because the challenges facing the agriculture industry are immense, the Budget prioritizes competitive research through the Department's flagship grant program, the Agriculture and Food Research Initiative (AFRI). The Budget requests $500 million for AFRI, an increase of $100 million above the 2018 enacted level, and maintains formula-based research and extension grants at the level requested in the 2019 Budget. In 2020, the Budget also invests in the Nation's aging research infrastructure by proposing $50 million for a new competitive grant program to modernize agriculture research facilities at land grant universities. The Budget proposes $1.2 billion for the Agricultural Research Service, which conducts in-house basic and applied research. This includes additional funding for the National Bio- and Agro-Defense Facility, currently under construction in Manhattan, Kansas. USDA is assuming the responsibility for operational planning and future operations of the facility, which will provide the United States the ability to conduct comprehensive research, develop vaccines, and provide enhanced diagnostic capabilities to protect against emerging foreign animal and zoonotic diseases that threaten the Nation's food supply, agricultural economy, and public health. The Budget also proposes $50 million for modernizing Agricultural Research Service facilities.

Implements Firefighting Funding Fix and Supports Forest Management Priorities. In 2018, Forest Service wildfire suppression spending was $2.6 billion, a record level for the second consecutive year. Extreme fire behavior fueled by dry forest ecosystems and aggressive suppression operations in the wildland-urban interface to protect life and property were primary factors contributing to this unprecedented outlay of resources. The Administration's work with the Congress to enact a wildfire funding fix culminated last March with the wildfire cap adjustment in the Consolidated Appropriations Act, 2018. In 2020, the wildfire cap adjustment would provide the Forest Service and the Department of the Interior with additional funding of up to $2.25 billion if the agencies fully expend their base funding levels for wildfire suppression. This funding aims to eliminate the need for disruptive "fire borrowing" from other uses to fund shortfalls during times of emergency.

In addition, the Administration has been direct and unequivocal about the need to accelerate active forest management. The Budget reflects this critical priority by requesting $450 million for hazardous fuel mitigation work and $375 million for the forest products program, higher amounts than in any prior Budget or enacted appropriation for both programs. Hazardous fuel removal is pivotal in ensuring Federal forests and watersheds are sustainable, healthy, and productive, which helps to make them safer and more resilient to the destructive impacts of wildfire. These programs also generate jobs in rural forest communities.

Improves Customer Service. The Budget supports new and continuing investments in information technology modernization by USDA to improve customer service and streamline and modernize rural and farm program and service delivery. Through the *https://www.Farmers.gov* service portal, the Department is working toward greater online service delivery and fewer in-person and paper-based transactions. In addition, the Budget continues support for the Secretary's realigned Farm Production and Conservation mission area by streamlining service delivery between the Farm Service Agency, Natural Resources Conservation Service, and Risk Management Agency to improve efficiency, effectiveness, and accountability.

Supports Comprehensive Farm Safety Net Reforms and Reduces Waste. The Budget proposes to optimize and improve crop insurance and commodity programs in a way that maintains a strong safety net. The Budget does this while also achieving savings, eliminating subsidies to higher income farmers, and reducing overly generous crop insurance premium subsidies to farmers and payments made to private sector insurance companies. The Budget includes a bold set of proposals, including those that would reduce the average premium subsidy for crop insurance from 62 percent to 48 percent and limit commodity, conservation, and crop insurance subsidies to those producers that have an Adjusted Gross Income of $500,000 or less. In addition, the Budget proposes reductions to overly generous subsidies provided to participating insurance companies by capping underwriting gains at 12 percent, which would ensure that the companies receive a reasonable rate of return given the risks associated with their participation in the crop insurance program. The Budget proposes to tighten commodity payment limits, including eliminating an unnecessary and separate payment limit for peanut producers and limiting eligibility for commodity subsidies to one manager per farm.

Ensures Commodity Purchases and Donations and Improves Program Transparency. During times of market disruption, low prices, or oversupply, USDA has the ability to purchase commodities from the marketplace and donate them to domestic feeding programs and soup kitchens. The Budget includes a suite of proposals to ensure stable historical levels of funding for all the nutrition programs that benefit from these activities while also increasing transparency and improving operational efficiency.

DEPARTMENT OF COMMERCE

Funding Highlights:

- The Department of Commerce (DOC) ensures fair and secure trade; provides data that empowers and informs American businesses and citizens; prevents U.S. technologies from being exploited, misused, or stolen through export controls and an effective system of patents and trademarks; and conducts foundational research and development.
- The Budget request for DOC prioritizes and protects investments in core Government functions such as preparing for the 2020 Decennial Census, providing the observational infrastructure and personnel to produce timely and accurate weather forecasts, and enforcing laws that promote fair and secure trade.
- The Budget requests $12.2 billion for DOC, a $1.0 billion or a 9.3-percent increase from the 2019 estimate.

The President's 2020 Budget:

The Budget continues to invest in critical priorities such as the 2020 Decennial Census, trade enforcement, intellectual property, weather and Earth observations, and spectrum management. In order to fund these priorities in a fiscally disciplined manner, the Budget reduces grant funding and consolidates or eliminates duplicative or unnecessary programs.

Supports a Fair, Modern, and Accurate 2020 Decennial Census. April 1, 2020, is Census Day and marks the culmination of nearly a decade of design, research, and testing to meet the Administration's goal of conducting a complete, accurate, and fair Decennial Census. Required every 10 years by the Constitution, the Decennial Census is responsible for the allocation of congressional representation and more than $675 billion of Federal funds to local communities. The 2020 Census will be the most modern census in the Nation's history, as households will have the choice to participate via the internet, telephone, or by paper. An accurate Decennial Census is imperative because of the role its data play in shaping and informing policymaking for the next decade. The Budget recognizes

Did you know?

The census is the Nation's largest peacetime mobilization of its workforce, an exercise that requires collaboration across Federal agencies, non-Federal organizations, State and local governments, and the public. These efforts help to ensure an accurate and complete count of U.S. residents as required by the Constitution every 10 years. To make this a success, the Census Bureau will recruit more than three million applicants between now and 2020.

the importance of the Census Bureau's mandate by supporting $7.2 billion in total budget authority in 2020.

> *"The era of economic surrender is over. From now on, we expect trading relationships to be fair and to be reciprocal."*
>
> President Donald J. Trump
> September 28, 2018

Promotes Free and Fair Trade. The Budget includes $16 million to support the President's robust trade agenda in order to protect critical elements of U.S economic security and level the playing field for American workers, farmers, and manufacturers. The Budget supports the implementation of the John S. McCain National Defense Authorization Act of 2019, which expanded the jurisdiction of the Committee on Foreign Investment in the United States and provided DOC with new responsibilities to identify emerging and foundational technologies that are essential to national security. The Budget also establishes a new initiative within the International Trade Administration to counter the circumvention or evasion of U.S. trade actions aimed at those who engage in unfair and illegal trade practices.

Supports America's Prominence in Critical Technologies. The Budget provides $688 million for the National Institute of Standards and Technology to conduct cutting-edge research, including quantum computing, artificial intelligence, and microelectronics. Together, these investments would drive innovation for national security and economic competitiveness. The Budget also provides $10 million to support functions assigned in the Administration's Space Policy Directives, including new capacity to manage commercial space traffic and provide real-time data to serve the civilian space sector. In addition, the Budget supports the application of innovative spectrum access techniques, spectrum sharing technologies, and spectrum leasing options to enable smarter and more efficient ways to leverage the Nation's valuable and finite spectrum resources. As part of the Administration's commitment to the Heartland, the Budget funds broadband mapping work to support ongoing efforts to increase the availability of affordable, reliable, and modern high-speed internet access in rural and underserved communities.

Protects Lives and Property with Weather Data. America's satellites are vital to keeping America safe and secure, providing space-based observations that improve the accuracy and timeliness of weather predictions. The Budget provides $1.2 billion in funding to support the development of these critical satellite systems, including polar weather satellites, space weather instruments, and satellite data collection systems. The Budget also includes funding to study how commercial technologies could be leveraged to help support future satellite architectures, assure data continuity, and reduce lifecycle costs. Funding these priorities reduces the risk of a weather satellite coverage gap, which would have devastating consequences for public safety and the national economy.

Improves the Delivery of America's Economic Statistics. The President and the Administration are changing a once-stagnant economy with pro-growth policies, and the Nation's economic data tells the story of this success. The Budget recognizes the importance of economic statistics for businesses and everyday citizens to make informed decisions and confidently invest in America's future. The Administration urges the Congress to consider the *Delivering Government Solutions in the 21st Century* plan's recommendation to consolidate critical economic statistics programs at Census, the Bureau of Economic Analysis, and the Bureau of Labor Statistics, making agency operations more efficient, improving products, and reducing respondent burden.

As part of the Administration's commitment to deploy effectively Government resources to the neediest communities, the Budget also provides funding to improve poverty measurement in America.

Supports Infrastructure Permitting. The Budget supports the ongoing, multi-agency work to streamline Federal permitting processes by increasing the National Oceanic and Atmospheric Administration's (NOAA) capacity to complete environmental reviews for permitting applications under the Endangered Species and Marine Mammal Protection Acts. Allocating additional funding to this initiative would allow NOAA to reduce the burden on the regulated community by providing more timely, consistent, and clear consultations and authorizations, resulting in faster reviews and a reduced backlog for permits, including those supporting energy, oil and gas, and transportation projects. This investment in America's future would contribute to prosperity and economic growth.

Eliminates Redundant, Ineffective, and Inefficient Programs. Americans deserve a Government that makes investments that are transparent, accountable, and provide the greatest return for their hard-earned tax dollars. The Budget eliminates the Economic Development Administration, which provides small grants with limited measurable impacts and duplicates other Federal programs. The Budget also proposes to eliminate funding for several lower priority NOAA grant and education programs, including Sea Grant, Coastal Zone Management Grants, and the Pacific Coastal Salmon Recovery Fund. These eliminations would allow NOAA to better target remaining resources to core missions and services. In addition, the Budget eliminates Federal funding for the Manufacturing Extension Partnership program, assuming its transition to solely non-Federal revenue sources, as originally intended when the program was established. The Budget also proposes the modernization of the Minority Business Development Agency, reforming its operations to expand its reach and better help meet its programmatic objective of helping minority businesses.

DEPARTMENT OF DEFENSE

Funding Highlights:

- The Department of Defense (DOD) provides the combat credible military capabilities needed to compete, deter, and if necessary, fight and win wars to protect the security of the United States.
- The Budget funds the National Defense Strategy to support DOD's three lines of effort: rebuilding readiness and lethality; strengthening alliances and partnerships; and improving performance and affordability through reform.
- The Budget requests $718 billion for DOD, a $33 billion or 5-percent increase from the 2019 enacted level.

The President's 2020 Budget:

The Budget provides the necessary resources for DOD to defend the homeland, remain the pre-eminent military power in the world, ensure balances of power in key regions remain in America's favor, and advance an international order that is most conducive to U.S. security and prosperity. The Budget enhances the military's readiness and lethality, prioritizing strategic competition with China and Russia. The Budget also sustains efforts to deter and counter rogue regimes such as North Korea and Iran, defeat terrorist threats, and consolidate gains in Iraq and Afghanistan through a resource-sustainable approach. DOD will increase the impact of its investments, as it rebuilds more lethal force, strengthens the network of allies and partners, and implements reform.

The Budget builds on steady gains that have restored military readiness, enhanced lethality, increased force size, and driven the Islamic State of Iraq and Syria (ISIS) out of territory it once held. On this foundation of strength, the Budget reflects the full integration of the National Defense Strategy across DOD, and supports dominance across all domains. The Budget provides the Army, Navy, Air Force, and Marine Corps the capabilities to bolster advantage in the air, on land, and at sea, leveraging advances in key technologies, including long-range precision fires, hypersonic missiles, and missile defense systems. For space, the Budget supports the creation of a new branch of the Armed Forces, the United States Space Force, and a new combatant command, U.S. Space Command, while the Space Development Agency, which is being established in 2019, fosters innovation. For cyber, the Budget continues to integrate efforts and operationalize U.S. cyber strategy, while scaling artificial intelligence throughout the Department. The Budget funds these advanced capabilities for the force needed to achieve the objectives in the National Defense Strategy. In 2020, the Budget funds an end strength of 2,140,300 active and reserve military personnel, buys 12 battle force ships and two large experimental unmanned surface ships, procures 110 fighter aircraft, and modernizes nearly two armored brigade combat teams.

Ensures the Readiness of U.S. Armed Forces. The Budget provides the resources necessary to continue rebuilding military readiness, which had been degraded by budget reductions imposed by the Budget Control Act and more than 17 years of warfighting. The Budget includes increased funding for the U.S. Army to modernize existing forces, provides additional training for soldiers to meet readiness goals by 2022, and increases readiness of security assistance brigades to train, advise, and enable foreign security forces to build partner capacity. The Budget funds continuing efforts to improve Navy and Marine Corps aviation readiness, with robust funding for maintenance, spare parts, and flying hours, while prioritizing close combat investments in lethality and enablers to provide every advantage to America's tactical warfighters. The Budget also funds ship depot maintenance and ship operations accounts to the maximum executable levels. In addition, the Budget funds Air Force flying hours to the maximum executable levels and continues to fund maintenance at a high level to achieve desired readiness gains, in addition to an aggressive program to recruit and retain additional pilots. The Budget also expands multiyear investments in training for high-end combat to ensure the United States remains able to defeat any adversary.

> *"My Administration's National Security Strategy lays out a strategic vision for protecting the American people and preserving our way of life, promoting our prosperity, preserving peace through strength, and advancing American influence in the world."*
>
> President Donald J. Trump
> December 18, 2017

Modernizes the Nuclear Deterrent. The return of great power competition demonstrates the need for flexible, adaptable, and resilient nuclear capabilities to keep America safe and secure. The Budget continues the Administration's implementation of the Nuclear Posture Review through investments in nuclear ballistic missile submarines, strategic bombers, nuclear air-launched cruise missiles, intercontinental ballistic missiles, and the associated nuclear command, control, and communications systems.

Pursues Technological Innovation for Decisive Military Advantage. The rapid advancement and proliferation of new technologies is changing the character of war. To prevent the erosion of the U.S. competitive military advantage, DOD is investing in new technologies to compete, deter, and if necessary, fight and win the wars of the future. The Budget's key areas of focus include autonomous systems, hypersonics, and artificial intelligence, including $208 million to scale DOD's Joint Artificial Intelligence Center. In addition, in 2020 the Army's newly formed Army Futures Command would be at full operating capability, designed to increase the efficiency of Army modernization, by leveraging technology across the enterprise and reducing development time. The Budget requests more than $59 billion in research, engineering, and prototyping activities to maintain the military's technological superiority and conventional overmatch against priority challenges.

Establishes the United States Space Force (USSF). The Budget supports the creation of USSF as the sixth branch of the Armed Forces. For the first time in 70 years, DOD will establish a new service to organize, train, and equip DOD's forces in order to protect and defend America's national interests in the fourth domain of warfare. The USSF will initially realign existing space forces and materiel from the military services and will scale up responsibly and deliberately over the next several years in order to address increasing threats and maintain strategic stability. The Budget provides funding to establish the USSF as a new service within the Department of the Air Force while continuing to accelerate the development and procurement of vital capabilities to the Joint Force, allies, and partners. Central to achieving this new acquisition paradigm is the Space Development

Agency, which is being established in 2019 under existing authorities to foster innovation by leveraging the thriving domestic commercial space sector. The Budget also supports U.S. Space Command as the newest Combatant Command, which will employ the forces and capabilities presented by the USSF.

Advances Airpower for the 21st Century. The Budget request supports the continued modernization of DOD's aircraft fleets to enable them to meet the challenges they will face in the contested environment of the future. The Air Force's tactical fighter investment program is focused on procuring the advanced F-35A stealth fighter while improving its fleet of current fighters such as the F-15 and F-16. The Navy and Marine Corps would also continue to procure their own variants of the F-35, as well as modernize their current F/A-18E/F fighters. In addition, the Budget continues to fund the development of the next generation stealth bomber and procurement of KC-46 aerial refueling tankers. These investment programs would ensure that DOD will be able to successfully counter the wide variety of threats that could be encountered in future combat situations.

Builds a More Lethal and Ready Navy. The Budget enhances lethality to meet the Nation's security challenges today while preparing for tomorrow. The Budget balances between modernization and readiness as well as capability and capacity. Notably, the Budget accelerates acquisition for several key systems, including Unmanned Undersea Vehicles, and invests in advanced tactical munitions, such as Tactical Tomahawks and the Standard Missile 6 Block 1B. The Budget also buys two large experimental unmanned surface ships and 12 battle force ships, including three guided missile destroyers, three fast attack submarines, and the first of a new class of guided missile frigates. The Budget also supports the Navy's recent innovative procurement of nuclear aircraft carriers, which should enable the shipbuilder to achieve unprecedented efficiencies from the construction of two ships.

Improves Ground Combat Lethality. The Budget invests in enhancements to close combat lethality of small infantry units, and the modernization of armored brigades. Most combat deaths suffered by infantry squads happen while engaging with the enemy at close range. The Budget makes investments in improved equipment and training to enhance the overmatch of Army, Marine Corps, and Special Operations small combat units. By investing in new weapons and body armor, warfighter recruitment and training, tactical communications and sensors, the Budget makes these front line units more lethal, resilient, and capable in a close combat environment. The Budget also accelerates the modernization of the Army's armored brigades to nearly seven over the five-year window while investing in the development of a next generation ground combat vehicle.

Strengthens Missile Defense. The Budget supports the President's commitment to expand and improve state-of-the-art missile defense systems as articulated in the recently released Missile Defense Review (MDR). The Budget sustains deployed missile defense assets, improves system reliability against today's threats, increases engagement capability and capacity, and makes strides to rapidly address the advanced threat. The Budget continues work to build a new missile field at Fort Greely, Alaska, with 20 silos and 20 additional Ground-Based Interceptors (GBIs) in support of the Administration's plans to increase the number of deployed GBIs to 64, to protect the homeland against North Korean and other intermediate- and long-range ballistic missile threats. In addition to enhancing current capabilities, the Budget embraces the MDR principles of exploring promising new technologies, including in space, and enhancing offensive capabilities to neutralize missile threats prior to launch during a conflict.

Invests in Cyber Activities. The Budget continues to place a high priority on cybersecurity and cyber operations by requesting more than $9.6 billion in 2020 to advance DOD's three primary cyber missions: safeguarding DOD's networks, information, and systems; supporting military commander objectives; and defending the Nation. This investment provides the resources necessary to grow the capacity of U.S. military cyber forces (including the recently elevated United States Cyber Command), invest in the cyber workforce, and continue to maintain the highest cybersecurity standards at DOD.

Continues to Promote Stability and Security in South Asia. The Budget furthers the U.S. goal of a stable and secure South Asia by supporting the Afghan government and security forces in their fight against jihadist terrorist organizations. The Budget requests funding for continued U.S. training and assistance for the Afghan National Defense and Security Forces and enables U.S. forces to conduct counterterrorism operations.

Secures the Enduring Defeat of ISIS, al Qaeda, and other Jihadist Terrorists. The Budget requests the funding necessary to ensure the lasting defeat of ISIS. Building on ISIS's territorial defeat in Iraq and the liberation of ISIS-controlled territory in Syria, DOD will continue to work with partner forces to destroy remnants of ISIS, strengthen border security, retain territorial control, and disrupt ISIS's capability to attack the U.S. homeland and America's allies. The Budget also requests funding for DOD to address the threat from ISIS branches outside Iraq and Syria, and to protect the United States against other terrorist threats.

Increases Compensation for Servicemembers and Supports Military Families. Military compensation must be competitive to recruit and retain the most qualified men and women to serve in an All-Volunteer Force. The Budget proposes a 2020 military pay raise of 3.1 percent—the largest increase in a decade. The Budget also requests funding for a full range of compensation programs, from monthly incentive pays to recently modernized retirement benefits. In addition, the Budget requests funding to continue important programs that improve the quality of life for military families, and ensure they receive the support they need throughout every stage of their family members' service.

Strengthens the Defense Industrial Base. In September 2018, DOD released a whole-of-Government report titled *Assessing and Strengthening the Manufacturing and Defense Industrial Base and Supply Chain Resiliency in the United States*, pursuant to Executive Order 13806. Following through on the report's recommendations, the Budget invests $286 million in DOD efforts to ensure a robust, resilient, secure, and ready manufacturing and defense industrial base. DOD's investments to implement this comprehensive, Government-wide effort demonstrate that manufacturing and the defense industrial base are vital not only to the Nation's economic security, but also to national security.

Reforms Business Practices for Greater Performance and Accountability. DOD continues to pursue management reforms to increase affordability and redirect savings to higher priorities. For example, DOD will continue achieving savings by reducing management overhead and the size of headquarters staff in 2020. DOD is also modernizing business processes and systems and eliminating duplication, which will yield significant savings and transparency, and improve decision support. In addition, the Department is looking holistically at contract management for services and commodities, to identify better approaches to demand management, requirements definition, and contracting strategies. DOD has also reviewed spending priorities in light of the new National Defense Strategy, and realigned funds from outdated legacy capability to better support the Department's lethality against near peer threats. In total, DOD achieved $4.7 billion in reform savings in 2017 and 2018 and is targeting $6 billion in savings in 2019. The objective is not simply savings over time, but a sustainable change in process and culture that will continue to ensure the most effective use of resources and increased lethality.

Audits the Department and Invests in Fixing Audit Findings. Better management begins with effective financial stewardship of taxpayer dollars. With more than $2.6 trillion in assets spread across 24 stand-alone reporting entities, the Department's recent full financial statement audit was DOD's first comprehensive audit and the largest ever undertaken by an agency of the U.S.

Government. Under the President's leadership, DOD continues to place a high priority on performing annual financial statement audits to bolster accountability and public confidence in the Department's fiscal discipline and to modernize its business practices and systems. The Department will address findings by holding the military departments and defense agencies accountable for the development and implementation of corrective actions, with a goal of meaningful, persistent progress toward a clean audit opinion. Armed with audit findings and remediation plans, DOD will leverage better data to inform decision-making, while enhancing internal controls and business procedures to improve efficiency and effectiveness.

DEPARTMENT OF EDUCATION

Funding Highlights:

- The Department of Education focuses its mission on supporting States and school districts in their efforts to provide high-quality education to the Nation's most vulnerable students, on streamlining and simplifying funding for college, and on expanding access to new postsecondary options.
- The Budget demonstrates fiscal discipline while maintaining funding for key K-12 education formula grants and making targeted investments in school safety, workforce development, teacher quality, and school choice.
- The Budget devotes an unprecedented level of resources to promoting school choice by proposing a Federal tax credit of up to $50 billion over 10 years for donations to scholarship programs for families of elementary and secondary students who are seeking State-defined public or private education options.
- The Budget ensures students can successfully pursue various pathways of postsecondary education and training by investing in career and technical education, streamlining and improving student loan repayment, increasing institutional accountability, and offering the opportunity to use Pell Grants for high-quality, short-term training.
- The Budget requests $62.0 billion for the Department of Education, an $8.5 billion or 12.0-percent decrease compared to the 2019 enacted level (including cancellations of Pell Grant unobligated balances). Excluding cancellations, the Budget requests a program level of $64.0 billion for the Department of Education, a $7.1 billion or 10.0-percent decrease compared to the 2019 enacted level.

The President's 2020 Budget:

The President's Budget achieves two equally important goals: fiscal discipline in discretionary spending and support for priorities that would improve the Nation's schools and make the United States stronger by preparing the workforce for the jobs of the 21st Century. The Budget reduces the Federal role in education, and prioritizes targeted investments in school safety, teacher quality, school choice, and workforce development. By modernizing U.S. education and training programs, the Budget would increase competition and transparency, reduce student debt, and ensure that what students are learning matches the needs of emerging industries. By increasing accountability for institutions of higher education and helping students complete postsecondary education more quickly, the Budget would help make higher education more affordable and protects both students and taxpayers. In addition, the Budget includes a Federal school choice tax credit to provide scholarships for both private schools and qualifying public education expenses. These policies would initiate tremendous strides toward the Administration's goal of providing all students with the opportunity to receive a high-quality education and achieve future success.

K-12 Education

The Budget request for elementary and secondary education reflects this Administration's continued commitment to providing States and school districts with the resources and flexibility to ensure that all children receive an excellent education. In addition, the Budget builds on the Administration's efforts to give families more choices for their children's education and to ensure that all students learn in safe and secure schools.

> *"Parents have the greatest stake in the outcome of their child's education. Accordingly, they should also have the power to make sure their child is getting the right education."*
>
> Betsy DeVos
> Secretary
> March 13, 2018

Ensures Families Have the Resources and Choices to Provide the Best Education for Their Children. Families should be empowered to decide which schools and academic supports are best for their children. That is why the Budget makes a first-of-its-kind proposal to equip families with the financial resources necessary to choose the education that best serves their children. The Budget proposes to make available annually $5 billion worth of tax credits for individual and corporate donations to State-authorized nonprofit education scholarship-granting organizations (SGOs). SGOs would use donated funds to provide families with scholarships or additional educational resources that can be used on a range of educational activities such as career and technical dual-enrollment programs, afterschool tutoring programs, tuition for private schools, courses not available in their assigned schools, special education services, and additional qualifying public education expenses. States would determine family eligibility requirements and allowable uses of scholarship funds. In addition to this historic Federal tax-credit scholarship proposal, the Budget provides over $650 million to support public school choice. The Budget requests $500 million to fund the opening and expansion of high-quality public charter schools and the financing of charter school facilities. The Budget also requests $107 million to expand magnet schools, which offer specialized curricula and instructional programming. In addition, the Budget invests $50 million in funding for districts participating in the Title I student-centered funding pilot. The pilot program would help districts transition to more transparent funding systems that enable Federal, State, and local funding to follow the student to the public school of his or her choice.

Supports High-Need Students through Essential Formula Grant Programs. The Budget invests $15.9 billion in Title I grants, maintaining a historic level of funding for a program that provides critically-important support to students in high-poverty schools. Title I serves approximately 25 million students in nearly 60 percent of all public schools, and is the foundation for the State-developed accountability systems under the Elementary and Secondary Education Act (ESEA). The Budget also proposes $1.4 billion for Impact Aid programs that support school districts that educate federally-connected children, such as those living on military bases and Indian lands. The Budget continues to maintain the Federal investment in the Individuals with Disabilities Education Act (IDEA) formula and discretionary grant programs. The Budget invests $13.2 billion for IDEA formula grants to States to support special education and early intervention services for more than seven million children with disabilities, and requests $226 million for discretionary grants to support research, demonstrations, technical assistance and dissemination, and personnel preparation and development.

Protects Students and Secures Schools. The Administration is committed to ensuring that students are able to learn in a safe and secure educational environment. After the tragedy in Parkland, Florida, the President established the Federal Commission on School Safety to assess and develop Federal, State, and local policy recommendations to help prevent violence in schools. The recommendations were published in December 2018. The Budget provides approximately $700 million, an increase of $354 million compared to the 2019 Budget, in Departments of Education, Justice, and Health and Human Services grants to give States and school districts resources to implement the Commission's recommendations, such as expanding access to mental healthcare, developing threat assessments, and improving school climate. At the Department of Education, the Budget requests $200 million for School Safety National Activities, which provide grants to States and school districts to develop school emergency operation plans, offer counseling and emotional support in schools with pervasive violence, and implement evidence-based practices for improving behavioral outcomes.

Invests in Innovation to Elevate the Teaching Profession. The Administration is committed to ensuring teachers have access to high-quality professional development opportunities that meet their individual needs. The Budget proposes $200 million for the Teacher and School Leader Incentive grant program to improve teacher induction and recognize and reward teaching excellence. The program would support performance-based compensation systems and human capital management systems that include either high-quality mentoring of novice teachers or increased compensation for effective teachers, particularly in high-need subjects such as science, technology, engineering, and mathematics (STEM) and coding. The Budget also includes $300 million for Education Innovation and Research to support a rigorously evaluated demonstration of empowering teachers to choose the individualized continuing education and training that contributes to their own professional growth and improved student outcomes. Within the program, the Budget proposes to pilot vouchers for teachers, enabling them to select training opportunities that are tailored to their unique needs.

Higher Education

The Budget continues support for Federal programs that: help prepare low-income and minority students for postsecondary education; target student financial aid to help students and families pay rising college costs; promote multiple pathways to obtaining family-sustaining careers; and strengthen postsecondary institutions serving large proportions of minority students. The Budget also includes proposals that would address student debt by simplifying student loan repayment and redirecting inefficiencies in the student loan program to prioritize debt relief for undergraduate borrowers. These proposals would support congressional efforts to modernize and reauthorize the Higher Education Act to be responsive to the needs of both students and employers. The Budget also addresses student debt and higher education costs while reducing the complexity of student financial aid.

Increases Institutional Accountability. Investing in higher education generally provides strong value for students and taxpayers. However, some postsecondary programs fail to deliver a quality education that enables students to repay Federal student loans—leaving borrowers and taxpayers holding the bill. A better system would require postsecondary institutions accepting taxpayer funds to share a portion of the financial responsibility associated with student loans. The Administration plans to work with the Congress to address these issues.

> *"If the Federal Government is going to subsidize student loans, it has a right to expect that colleges work hard to control costs and invest their resources in their students. If colleges refuse to take this responsibility seriously, they will be held accountable ... And we must hold all schools equally accountable for their performance."*
>
> President Donald J. Trump
> as Presidential Candidate
> October 13, 2016

Reforms Student Loan Programs. In recent years, income-driven repayment (IDR) plans, which offer student borrowers the option of making affordable monthly payments based on factors such as income and family size, have grown in popularity. However, the numerous IDR plans currently offered to borrowers overly complicate choosing and enrolling in the right repayment plan. The Budget proposes to streamline student loan repayment by consolidating multiple IDR plans into a single plan. The Single IDR plan would cap a borrower's monthly payment at 12.5 percent of discretionary income. For undergraduate borrowers, any balance remaining after 180 months of repayment would be forgiven. For borrowers with any graduate debt, any balance remaining after 30 years of repayment would be forgiven.

To support this generous pathway to debt relief for all undergraduate borrowers, the Budget eliminates the Public Service Loan Forgiveness program, establishes reforms to guarantee that all borrowers in IDR pay an equitable share of their income, and eliminates subsidized loans. To further improve and simplify loan repayment, the Budget proposes auto-enrolling severely delinquent borrowers and instituting a process for borrowers to consent to share income data for multiple years. To facilitate these program improvements and to reduce improper payments, the Budget proposes to streamline the Department of Education's ability to verify applicants' income data held by the Internal Revenue Service. These reforms would reduce inefficiencies and waste in the student loan program, and focus assistance on needy undergraduate student borrowers. All student loan proposals would apply to loans originating on or after July 1, 2020, except those provided to borrowers to finish their current course of study.

Continues Investment in the NextGen Servicing and Processing Environment. The Budget invests $1.8 billion in Student Aid Administration at Federal Student Aid (FSA), which has 42 million customers and manages one of the largest consumer loan portfolios in the United States. Nearly 6,000 institutions of higher education participate in the Federal student aid programs. FSA's customers deserve a world-class experience, but they do not consistently receive one today. Currently, when customers apply for, receive, and repay Federal student aid, they interface with multiple brands and vendors. FSA is investing in best-in-class financial services technologies to deploy a mobile-first, mobile-complete digital customer experience. This transformation will provide better outcomes for customers, streamline processes and procedures for FSA employees, and improve value for American taxpayers.

Expands Pell Grant Eligibility for Short-Term Programs. There are many paths to a successful career in addition to a four-year degree. The Budget expands Pell Grant eligibility to include high-quality short-term programs. This would help more Americans access education and training programs that can equip them with skills to secure well-paying jobs in high-demand fields more quickly than traditional two-year or four-year degree programs.

Advances Grantmaking and Supports for Minority-Serving Institutions (MSIs) and Historically Black Colleges and Universities (HBCUs). The Budget supports important investments in the academic quality, institutional management and capacity, infrastructure, and student support services for MSIs and HBCUs. In particular, the Budget proposes to improve grantmaking by consolidating six MSI programs into a $148 million formula grant, providing funds more institutions can count on and yielding program management efficiencies. The Budget also continues to recognize the extraordinary contributions of HBCUs and requests more than $404 million to maintain funding for HBCU formula and competitive grant programs that strengthen their capacity to provide the highest quality education.

Empowers States to Deliver Evidence-Based Postsecondary Preparation Programs. The Budget proposes to restructure and streamline the TRIO and GEAR UP programs by consolidating them into a $950 million State formula grant. These grants would support evidence-based postsecondary preparation programs designed to help low-income students progress through the pipeline from middle school to postsecondary opportunities. Given the statutory prohibition limiting the Department's ability to evaluate overall TRIO program effectiveness using the most rigorous methodologies, as well as budget constraints, the Budget supports a restructuring of the programs that leverages evidence-based activities and allows States more flexibility in meeting the unique needs of their students.

Workforce

In today's rapidly changing economy, it is more important than ever to prepare workers to fill both existing and future jobs. The Administration has placed a priority on science, technology, and computer science skills, devoting a minimum of $200 million annually to prepare students, especially girls and minorities who are underrepresented in these industries, for the growing role technology is playing in driving the American economy. These skills open the door to jobs and drive solutions to complex problems across industries. The U.S. education system must provide access to affordable and quality education and training that includes in-demand career and vocational tracks as well as opportunities for work-based and experiential learning. The Budget supports programs that help students obtain the skills necessary to secure high-paying jobs in today's workforce and contribute to the Nation's economy.

Invests in Career and Technical Education (CTE). As part of the Administration's commitment to ensuring the Nation's students have the knowledge and skills to succeed in today's competitive economy, the Budget includes $1.3 billion for CTE State grants. The recently reauthorized program helps ensure students have access to technical education, including work-based learning during high school and a wide array of post-secondary options including certificate programs, community colleges, and apprenticeships. The Budget also includes $20 million for CTE National Programs to support quality STEM and coding-focused CTE programs. In addition, the Budget proposes to double the American Competitiveness and Workforce Improvement Act fee for the H-1B visa program and direct 15 percent of the revenues to the CTE State grants.

Refocuses Federal Work Study to Emphasize Workforce Development. The Budget proposes to reform the Federal Work Study program to support workforce and career-oriented training opportunities for low-income undergraduate students, not just subsidized employment as a means of financial aid, in order to create more available pathways to high-paying jobs. The program would allocate funds to schools based in part on enrollment of Pell recipients. Schools could fund individual students through subsidized employment, paid internships, or other designs, as long as the placements were career or academically relevant. Schools could also serve groups of students through programs and initiatives that expose students to or build their preparedness for careers.

Reduces Waste: Eliminates Ineffective or Redundant Programs. The Budget eliminates funding for 29 discretionary programs that do not address national needs, duplicate other programs, are ineffective, are poorly targeted, or are more appropriately supported by State, local, or private funds. These eliminations would decrease taxpayer costs by $6.7 billion and include the Supporting Effective Instruction State Grants, 21st Century Community Learning Centers, and Federal Supplemental Educational Opportunity Grants.

DEPARTMENT OF ENERGY

Funding Highlights:

- The mission of the Department of Energy (DOE) is to advance U.S. national security and economic growth through transformative science and technology innovations that promotes affordable and reliable energy through market solutions, and meets America's nuclear security and environmental clean-up challenges.
- The 2020 Budget makes strategic investments to maintain global leadership in scientific and technological innovation and aggressively modernize the nuclear security enterprise that underpins the safety and security of Americans both at home and abroad.
- The 2020 Budget requests $31.7 billion for DOE, an 11-percent decrease from the 2019 enacted level.

The President's 2020 Budget:

The Budget for DOE enables advancement of American leadership in science and technology, a cornerstone to enhancing national security, economic growth, and job creation. American ingenuity combined with free-market capitalism can drive tremendous technological breakthroughs. The Budget reasserts that the proper role of the Federal Government is to focus resources on early-stage research and development (R&D) of energy technologies. Refocusing on the appropriate role of the Federal Government ensures that taxpayer dollars are being effectively used while implementing fiscal discipline.

The Budget addresses the challenges that face the Nation and reflects the critical role DOE has in protecting the safety and security of the American people, including by ensuring that nuclear and radiological materials worldwide remain secured against theft by those who might use them against the U.S. homeland or U.S. interests abroad. The Budget also funds the modernization of nuclear weapons and ensures that the U.S. nuclear force remains superior in the world. In addition, the Budget ensures continued progress on cleaning up sites contaminated from nuclear weapons production and nuclear energy R&D. The Budget also demonstrates the Administration's commitment to nuclear waste management by supporting the implementation of a robust interim storage program and restarting the Nuclear Regulatory Commission licensing proceeding for the Yucca Mountain geologic repository.

The Budget further protects taxpayers by eliminating costly, wasteful or duplicative programs. The private sector is better positioned to provide financing for the deployment of commercially viable projects. As a result, programs proposed for elimination include: the Title XVII Innovative Technology Loan Guarantee Program; the Advanced Technology Vehicle Manufacturing Loan

Program; and the Tribal Energy Loan Guarantee Program. To further achieve fiscal discipline and reduce taxpayer risk, the Budget proposes to repeal the Western Area Power Administration's borrowing authority that finances the construction of electricity transmission projects. Investments in transmission assets are best carried out by the private sector where there are appropriate market and regulatory incentives. To promote effective and efficient use of taxpayer funds, the Advanced Research Projects Agency-Energy (ARPA-E) is also proposed for elimination. This elimination facilitates opportunities to integrate the positive aspects of ARPA-E into DOE's applied energy research programs. In addition, the elimination enables the Department to efficiently direct scarce resources as part of an integrated national energy strategy.

Modernizes the Nuclear Deterrent. The Budget supports the Administration's Nuclear Posture Review by maintaining a tailored and flexible nuclear deterrent that protects the homeland, assures allies, and, above all, deters adversaries. While the investments in America's nuclear weapons are large, given their importance in keeping America safe, the investments should be regarded as both necessary and affordable. The Budget increases investments in the nuclear stockpile to guarantee it is modern, robust, safe, and effective. Specifically, the Budget completes development and production of the W76-2 warhead, begins production of the B61-12 and the W88 Alteration 370, and continues development of the W80-4 and the W87-1. The Budget also continues support of the underlying Stockpile Stewardship Program, which facilitates stockpile modernization while advancing scientific understanding that can be applied to other national security missions.

Rebuilds Nuclear Weapons Infrastructure. The National Nuclear Security Administration's (NNSA) nuclear security enterprise of national laboratories, production plants, and the Nevada National Security Site is a critical component of the U.S. nuclear deterrent. However, the physical infrastructure is in acute need of updating to better support the stockpile, as more than half the facilities are over 40 years old. To maintain a modern, resilient infrastructure, the Nation must invest in facilities needed to produce strategic materials and components for U.S. nuclear weapons. The Budget makes these significant investments, such as construction of the Uranium Processing Facility in Tennessee. The Budget also increases funding to repurpose the Mixed-Oxide (MOX) Fuel Fabrication Facility in South Carolina for production of nuclear weapons plutonium pits to meet Department of Defense requirements. NNSA must have a modern enterprise with the capacity to respond to unforeseen developments.

Reduces Global Nuclear Threats. Nuclear terrorism and proliferation remain serious threats to the security of the United States and its allies. The Nation must maintain vigilance in its nuclear nonproliferation, counter-proliferation, and counterterrorism efforts to provide for the safety and security of the American people. The Budget makes the necessary, fiscally disciplined investments in these capabilities. Specifically, the Budget supports enhanced capabilities within the United States to respond more quickly to a nuclear terrorism threat. The Budget continues efforts to prevent terrorists from acquiring nuclear materials by removing these materials from around the world and helping countries protect remaining materials.

Disposes of Surplus Plutonium. With the termination of the MOX project, the Budget aggressively moves forward with the Dilute and Dispose approach to disposing of surplus plutonium. Consistent with the Administration's commitments to South Carolina, the Budget expedites removal of plutonium from the State. The Budget also makes investments in key facilities at the Savannah River Site and the Los Alamos National Laboratory to further accelerate plutonium disposition.

Provides Safe Naval Nuclear Propulsion. The Budget continues DOE's support of a strong U.S. Navy through NNSA's Naval Reactors (NR) program. NR works to provide the U.S. Navy with safe, environmentally conscious operation of nuclear propulsion plants for submarines and aircraft carriers. The Budget continues development of the reactor systems for the *Columbia*-class ballistic missile submarine, maintaining alignment with the Navy for lead ship delivery. The Budget also supports recapitalization of the Navy's spent fuel handling infrastructure while making other needed investments at the four Naval Nuclear Laboratory sites.

Supports Cutting-Edge Basic Research and Leading Scientific User Facilities. The Budget provides $5.5 billion for the Office of Science to continue its mission to focus on early-stage research, operate the national laboratories, and continue high priority construction projects. Within this amount, $500 million is budgeted for Exascale computing to help secure a global leadership role in supercomputing, $169 million for Quantum Information Science, $71 million for artificial intelligence and machine learning, and $25 million to enhance materials and chemistry foundational research to support U.S.-based leadership in microelectronics.

Invests in Laboratory Infrastructure and Testbeds to Enable Future Breakthroughs in Energy. DOE supports 17 national laboratories that offer world class scientific user facilities and the critical laboratory infrastructure necessary to operate them. Within the Office of Science, Science Laboratory Infrastructure focuses on strengthening the backbone of the labs with $118 million to modernize aging critical infrastructure and laboratory space. The Budget continues to ensure access to the scientific user facilities of the future, including $104 million for the Long Baseline Neutrino Facility/Deep Underground Neutrino Experiment and $40 million to complete the Facility for Rare Isotope Beams. The Budget prioritizes select infrastructure and testbeds to maintain the world-class nature of national laboratory facilities and better enable private sector demonstration and deployment of energy technologies. For example, the Budget includes $100 million to put DOE on a path to construct the Versatile Advanced (Fast) Test Reactor, a facility that would enable development and testing of advanced fuels and materials for the next generation of commercial nuclear reactors. The Budget also includes $5 million for a new Grid Storage Launchpad initiative, which would support a new lab-based grid-scale battery testing center to help push technologies forward, and $15 million to accelerate the conversion of the National Wind Testing Facility site into an experimental microgrid capable of testing grid integration at the megawatt scale.

Enhances Support for Cyber and Energy Security Initiatives. Ranging from cybersecurity of the bulk electrical system to prioritization of early-stage R&D focused on hardening energy infrastructure, the Budget prioritizes energy security for all Americans through continued investments that address the many cyber threats across the Nation's energy sector. To ensure robust cybersecurity programs across the energy sector, the Budget provides funding in multiple programs, including over $156 million for the recently established Office of Cybersecurity, Energy Security, and Emergency Response. This funding would support early-stage R&D activities that improve cybersecurity and resilience to enable the private sector to harden and evolve critical infrastructure, including protecting critical infrastructure from both natural and man-made events.

Launches an Era of Energy Dominance through Strategic Support for Energy Technology Innovation. The United States has among the most abundant and diverse energy resources in the world, including oil, gas, coal, nuclear, and renewables. The ability of entrepreneurs and businesses to commercialize technologies that take full advantage of those resources is paramount to promoting U.S. economic growth, security, and competitiveness. That is why the Budget provides a programmatic funding level of $2.3 billion across the applied energy programs at DOE to support early-stage R&D that will enable the private sector to

> *"America's future has never been brighter, and American energy is leading the way in providing jobs, opportunity, and security for our Nation."*
>
> President Donald J. Trump
> September 28, 2018

deploy the next generation of technologies and energy services that usher in a more secure, resilient, and integrated energy system.

The Budget emphasizes two new intra-departmental initiatives within the Applied Energy Office portfolio that coordinate and build upon existing capabilities and expertise and seek to replicate successful program models to achieve results more effectively. Specifically, the Budget requests $158 million for the Advanced Energy Storage Initiative, a coordinated effort jointly led by the Office of Electricity and the Office of Energy Efficiency and Renewable Energy (EERE) to advance energy storage R&D as a key to increasing energy security, reliability, and resilience. The initiative takes a broad, holistic view of energy storage as a set of capabilities that enable the conversion of energy resources to useful energy services. Assuring grid security and resilience will require greater grid flexibility and the deployment of grid assets, such as energy storage, that can efficiently buffer increased variable supply and demand. The Budget also requests $59 million for the Harsh Environment Materials Initiative, a coordinated effort led by the Office of Nuclear Energy and the Office of Fossil Energy, in coordination with the Advanced Manufacturing Office within EERE, to exploit synergies in materials and component manufacturing R&D for advanced thermoelectric power plants. This initiative leverages activities related to advanced reactor technologies and high efficiency low emissions modular coal plants to align the R&D of novel materials, integrated sensors, and manufacturing processes relevant for advanced thermoelectric power plants.

Continues Reforms in the Environmental Management Program to Address the Challenge of Waste and Contamination from Nuclear Weapons Production. The Budget includes $6.5 billion for 16 sites remaining to be cleaned up to meet environmental regulatory requirements. The Budget provides within this total $128 million to advance the initiative to accelerate deactivation and decommissioning of selected high-risk excess facilities to protect human health and the environment, and to support the modernization of the Nuclear Security Enterprise.

Proposes to Divest Federally Owned and Operated Transmission Assets and Authorize the Power Marketing Administrations (PMAs) to Charge Market Based Rates for Power. The Budget proposes to sell the transmission assets owned and operated by the PMAs, including those of Southwestern Power Administration, Western Area Power Administration, and Bonneville Power Administration. The Budget also proposes to authorize the PMAs to charge rates comparable to those charged by for-profit, investor-owned utilities, rather than being limited to cost-based rates, for electricity. The vast majority of the Nation's electricity needs are met through investor-owned utilities. Reducing or eliminating the Federal Government's role in electricity transmission infrastructure ownership, thereby increasing the private sector's role, and introducing more market-based incentives, including rates, for power sales from Federal dams would encourage a more efficient allocation of economic resources and mitigate risk to taxpayers.

DEPARTMENT OF HEALTH AND HUMAN SERVICES

Funding Highlights:

- The mission of the Department of Health and Human Services (HHS) is to protect and strengthen the health and well-being of Americans through effective health and human services for the American people and by fostering sound, sustained advances in the sciences underlying medicine, public health, and social services.
- The Budget addresses the Nation's critical public health needs through investments that combat the opioid epidemic and support mental health services, increase efforts to eliminate infectious diseases, support high priority biomedical research, speed access to new innovative technology, and enhance emergency preparedness and health security. The Budget also offers strategies to reduce drug-related costs, improve the health of older Americans, and strengthen work requirements to promote self-sufficiency.
- The Budget also invests in child care to support America's working families, and promotes work among able-bodied adults receiving assistance.
- The 2020 Budget requests $87.1 billion for HHS, a 12-percent decrease from the 2019 estimated level. The Budget proposes $1,248.8 billion in net mandatory health savings, reducing longer-term deficits.

The President's 2020 Budget:

The Budget supports the mission of HHS while creating a streamlined Federal Government that promotes the most efficient and effective use of taxpayer dollars. The Budget invests in the highest priority public health needs of the Nation—combatting the opioid epidemic, supporting services for serious mental illness, and preparing for public health threats. The Budget launches an initiative to end HIV/AIDS in America, an ambitious, yet necessary effort to eliminate a disease that has plagued the Nation for more than three decades. In addition, the Budget takes bold steps to increase access and reduce drug costs for Americans, empowers consumers and States to regain control over healthcare and increase affordability and consumer choice, and strengthens and protects the Medicare program for America's seniors.

Combats the Opioid Epidemic. In addition to progress already being made by the Administration, the Budget makes significant investments to combat the drug abuse and opioid epidemic, which claimed more than 70,000 lives in 2017. In the last year, the President released a new Initiative to Stop Opioid Abuse and Reduce Drug Supply and Demand, secured $6 billion in new resources in the 2018 and 2019 to combat the epidemic, and signed the SUPPORT for Patients and Communities

Act, which enhances the Federal response to the opioid epidemic. The number of opioid prescriptions dispensed monthly has fallen by more than 20 percent since the beginning of 2017 and preliminary data from the Centers for Disease Control and Prevention (CDC) suggests that the number of drug overdose deaths are finally starting to level off or even decline.

The Budget sustains critical investments in surveillance, prevention, treatment, access to overdose reversal drugs, recovery support services, and research. For example, the Budget includes $1.5 billion for State Opioid Response grants, which fund prevention, treatment, and recovery support services in all States and Territories. The Budget maintains more than $1 billion in the National Institutes of Health (NIH) for opioid and pain research, including the continuation of the Helping to End Addiction Long-term Initiative that began in 2018.

The Budget includes $221 million to expand the behavioral health workforce, including an additional $4 million for a new effort authorized in the SUPPORT for Patients and Communities Act to increase the number of providers that are able to prescribe medication-assisted treatment. In addition, the Budget maintains $120 million to support treatment and prevention of substance use disorder, including opioid abuse, in rural communities at the highest risk. The Budget also enables States to more easily provide one year of post-partum Medicaid coverage for women with a substance use disorder, to improve health outcomes for mothers and their infants.

The Budget provides $476 million for CDC to continue current activities in support of all 50 States and Territories, as well as local jurisdictions, to track and prevent overdose deaths. CDC would prioritize expanding support to States and Territories to collect and report real-time overdose and robust overdose mortality data. The Budget also provides $58 million for CDC to address the infectious disease consequences of the opioid epidemic. Approximately 95 percent of new Hepatitis C infections and one of every seven new HIV infections is due to injection drug use. CDC would focus on areas most at risk for outbreaks of HIV and hepatitis due to injection drug use.

Addresses Mental Health Needs. Mental illness, especially serious mental illness, takes a toll on individuals, families, and communities all across the United States. In 2017, only 7.5 million of the 11.2 million adults suffering from serious mental illness received mental health services in the past year. The Budget invests in activities that increase access to mental health services. The Budget includes $723 million for the Community Mental Health Services Block Grant, which provides funding to every State to provide services to seriously mentally ill adults and children with serious emotional disturbances, and $150 million for Certified Community Behavioral Health Centers, which provide comprehensive healthcare services, including 24-hour crisis response services to individuals with serious mental illness. The Budget also makes new targeted investments to help divert seriously mentally ill individuals away from the criminal justice system and into treatment, and to increase the access to evidence-based comprehensive services. In addition, the Budget contains important investments for children and young adults, including $125 million for Children's Mental Health Services and $133 million for school violence prevention. The Budget funds important suicide prevention activities, such as the suicide lifeline and activities to address the high suicide rates in middle-age and older adults.

Reforms Drug Pricing and Payment. The Administration's comprehensive drug pricing strategy addresses the problem of high drug prices, provides greater access to lifesaving medical products, and ensures that the United States remains the leader in biomedical innovation. Consistent with the Administration's *American Patients First Blueprint,* the Budget proposes strategies targeted at increasing competition, encouraging better negotiation, incentivizing lower list prices, and lowering out-of-pocket costs for beneficiaries.

- Modernizes the Medicare Part D Prescription Drug Benefit—In the past year, the Administration made great strides to better equip plans with the tools necessary to manage drug spending in the Part D program. The Budget builds on this progress by addressing the misaligned incentives of the Part D benefit structure. The proposed changes are designed to: encourage utilization of higher value drugs by eliminating cost-sharing for generic drugs for beneficiaries who receive the low-income subsidy; remove the competitive disadvantage placed on generic drugs that increases spending for both beneficiaries and the Government; and provide beneficiaries with more predictable annual drug expenses through the creation of a new out-of-pocket spending cap.

> *"One of my greatest priorities is to reduce the price of prescription drugs. In many other countries, these drugs cost far less than what we pay in the United States. That is why I have directed my Administration to make fixing the injustice of high drug prices one of our top priorities. Prices will come down."*
>
> President Donald J. Trump
> January 30, 2018

- Reduces Costs for Part B Drugs—The Budget addresses unnecessary barriers to free-market competition in Part B and proposes reforms to payment for Part B drugs, which heavily influences physician-prescribing behavior. Longstanding challenges in Part B include the lack of competition among drugs with similar health effects and limited tools to encourage lower drug prices. To address these challenges, the Budget includes proposals targeted at: removing the three-year payment protection of average sales price (ASP) plus six percent for certain new drugs provided in outpatient hospitals; deterring anti-competitive behavior from drug manufacturers that exploit aspects of the patent system to keep out competition; and moving coverage of some Part B drugs to Part D to reduce spending while protecting beneficiaries from increased out of pocket costs.

  In addition, the Budget limits growth in Part B drug payment to an inflation benchmark and mandates manufacturers report ASP data for all Part B drugs to improve payment accuracy. The Budget also modifies hospitals' payment for drugs acquired through the 340B drug discount program by rewarding hospitals that provide charity care and reducing payments to hospitals that provide little to no charity care.

- Increases Access to More Affordable Generics Through Greater Competition—The Budget would include a number of proposals to speed development of generics and eliminate loopholes that have allowed drug companies to use the regulatory framework to hinder competition. The Budget would:

  - Reform the current 180-day exclusivity forfeiture provision for first generics so that first generics do not block subsequent generics from U.S. Food and Drug Administration (FDA) approval.

  - Clarify FDA's approach in determining whether a new drug is a new chemical entity to ensure that only truly innovative new drugs receive an additional five years of exclusivity.

  - Enhance FDA authority to address abuse of petition process so FDA has greater flexibility to summarily deny petitions when circumstances indicate that the primary purpose of the petition is to delay FDA approval.

  - Enable FDA to tentatively approve a subsequent generic application, which would start the 180-day exclusivity clock, when a first to file generic application cannot be approved due to deficiencies.

- Improves Program Integrity—The Budget proposes to improve the integrity of the 340B program and ensure that benefits are used to help low-income and uninsured patients. This proposal includes broad regulatory authority for the 340B Drug Pricing Program to set enforceable standards of program participation and requires all covered entities to report on use of program savings.

- Lowers Costs and Increases Flexibility for Medicaid Prescription Drugs—The Budget proposes removing the cap on Medicaid manufacturer drug rebates, to ensure rebates reflect all price increases for a drug. In addition, the Budget includes new demonstration authority allowing States to test innovative approaches for Medicaid prescription drug coverage. Under the demonstration, participating States would test a closed formulary and negotiate prices directly with manufacturers. The Budget also prevents manufacturers from using authorized generics to lower their rebate obligations, and includes payment changes so State Medicaid programs do not overpay for generic drugs, saving money for States and taxpayers.

> *"[U]nder this Administration, we are putting American patients first...I've instructed Secretary Azar to begin moving forward on reforms that will bring soaring drug prices back down to earth."*
>
> President Donald J. Trump
> May 11, 2018

Empowers States and Consumers to Reform Healthcare. Under the Patient Protection and Affordable Care Act (PPACA) healthcare spending has increased significantly, particularly premiums for families without employer-sponsored coverage who don't qualify for Obamacare subsidies. To help expand families' health coverage options, the President signed into law the Tax Cut and Jobs Act, which eliminated Obamacare's individual mandate penalty, and took swift administrative actions that empower individuals to purchase health coverage that best suits their needs. Some new flexibilities already implemented include expanding access to Association Health Plans for employers and many self-employed individuals, extending the duration and renewability of Short-Term Limited Duration Insurance, and proposing to allow employers to offer health reimbursement arrangements to employees for purchasing individual market coverage.

The Budget supports several initiatives to empower States and consumers to regain control over healthcare and increase affordability and consumer choice. The proposals in the Budget strive to put States back into the healthcare driver's seat as States are best situated to make decisions to improve the health and healthcare delivery of their citizens.

First, the Budget continues to support a two-part approach, starting with enactment of legislation modeled after the Graham-Cassidy-Heller-Johnson bill proposed in September 2017, followed by enactment of additional reforms to help set Government healthcare spending on a sustainable fiscal path that leads to higher value spending. Beginning in 2021, the Market-Based Health Care Grant Program, the Medicaid block grant, and the per capita cap program are set to grow at the Consumer Price Index. These programs would support States as they transition to more sustainable healthcare programs and encourage States to pursue innovative ideas that aim to curb costs moving forward. The Budget acknowledges the importance of ensuring protections for individuals with pre-existing conditions and States would be required to include such plans in their applications for these grants. Specifically, States would be required to allocate at least 10 percent of their grant funding to be used to ensure protections for high-cost individuals, including those with pre-existing conditions. States would have the flexibility to design an approach that best allows States to meet this goal. The two-part approach would also provide relief for States and consumers from many of the PPACA's insurance rules and pricing restrictions that have resulted in a lack of affordable coverage options. This new flexibility would build on the Administration's regulatory actions and would empower more people to buy insurance plans that work for them, a substantial benefit to middle class families who do not receive coverage through the workplace or do not qualify for subsidies.

The Budget also proposes to give States additional flexibility over their Medicaid programs by transferring control of Medicaid transformation efforts locally where it belongs. The Administration recognizes that the only way to reform Medicaid and set it on a sound fiscal path is by putting States on equal footing with the Federal Government to implement comprehensive Medicaid financing reform through a per capita cap or block grant. A new Federal-State partnership is necessary to eliminate inefficient Medicaid spending, including repeal of the Medicaid expansion, and reducing financing gimmicks such as provider taxes. The Budget would empower States to design State-based solutions that prioritize Medicaid dollars for the most vulnerable and support innovation.

The Budget emboldens individuals to take charge of their healthcare needs and own their healthcare spending, while protecting them from large unexpected costs. Currently, too many Americans are gouged by unfair and often surprise bills for hospital care and for pharmaceutical drugs. The President is committed to addressing this issue and proposes that the Congress partner in these efforts to increase healthcare price transparency of providers, suppliers, and insurers, including curtailing surprise medical bills. This would not only help protect consumers from unexpected healthcare costs, but would also empower them to make more informed healthcare decisions. Such price transparency may lead to more robust competition between actors in the healthcare supply chain, ultimately lowering costs for patients and plan sponsors such as employers, associations, and unions. To further encourage increased consumer engagement, the Budget immediately requires all subsidized individuals that purchase health coverage on the Federal Exchange to contribute something to their healthcare coverage.

Health savings accounts (HSAs) are a tool to increase consumer engagement and lower healthcare spending without negatively affecting quality. The Budget includes a series of reforms to expand access to HSAs. Under tax provisions originally enacted in 2003, persons enrolled in certain high deductible health plans—which are generally referred to here as HSA-qualified plans—may contribute to savings accounts to pay for healthcare expenses on a tax-preferred basis. The Budget proposes that all plans with an actuarial value of up to 70 percent may be integrated with HSAs. This would enable consumers to utilize the benefits of HSAs with a larger number of innovative plan designs.

Together, these reforms and consumer protections aim to encourage innovation from States, help consumers with the costs of their healthcare, and focus Medicaid resources on the most vulnerable individuals, while continuing to protect those with high healthcare needs.

Modernizes Medicaid to Enhance State Flexibility. The Budget would empower States with additional tools to strengthen their Medicaid programs and empower States to further modernize Medicaid benefits and eligibility. The Budget would give States additional flexibility around benefits and cost-sharing, such as increasing copayments for non-emergency use of the emergency department to encourage appropriate use of healthcare resources, as well as allowing States to consider savings and other assets when determining Medicaid eligibility. In addition, the Budget would allow States to streamline appeals processes and delegate authority to another entity, to help eliminate duplicative appeals and reduce beneficiary confusion. The Budget would also bolster the safety net available to

States experiencing Children's Health Insurance Program (CHIP) funding shortfalls, while eliminating funding streams that do not support children's health.

Reduces Wasteful Medicaid Spending. The Budget takes numerous steps to reduce wasteful Medicaid spending. The Budget proposes eliminating loopholes that some States use to shift and increase costs to Federal taxpayers, and for the Centers for Medicare and Medicaid Services (CMS) to issue guidance ensuring that State Medicaid supplemental payments to hospitals and other providers are supported by robust and timely data. The Budget also proposes realigning the Federal matching payments for State Medicaid eligibility workers with other administrative costs, providing a fair balance between Federal and State resources for these activities. In addition, the Budget extends current law reductions in Medicaid disproportionate share hospital payments, and proposes to limit reimbursement to Government providers to no more than the cost of providing services to Medicaid beneficiaries.

Improves Program Integrity for Medicare, Medicaid, and CHIP. The Budget includes several legislative proposals and administrative actions to reduce monetary loss from improper payments and strengthen the integrity and sustainability of Medicare, Medicaid, and CHIP. Combined with additional funding investments in the Health Care Fraud and Abuse Control program, these policies provide CMS with additional resources and tools to combat waste, fraud, and abuse and to promote high-quality and efficient healthcare.

The Budget proposes to expand the Medicare program's authority to conduct prior authorization on items or services at high risk of fraud and abuse. The proposal helps ensure that the right payment goes to the right provider for appropriate services and saves taxpayer dollars from paying for Medicare services that are not medically necessary. The Budget also addresses healthcare overutilization and waste by expanding CMS's work in notifying providers that prescribe drugs or perform procedures in excess of their peers. In addition, the Budget proposes to strengthen Medicare Advantage program integrity by ensuring initial risk-adjustment payments are paid correctly and expanding risk-adjustment data validation audits.

Addressing vulnerabilities to Medicaid program integrity is a key priority for the Administration, and the Budget includes a number of proposals to ensure sound stewardship and oversight of Medicaid resources. For example, the Budget proposes to strengthen CMS's ability to partner with States to address improper payments and ensure Federal recovery of incorrect eligibility determinations, an area of concern identified by the HHS Office of Inspector General. In addition, the Budget allows States flexibility to more frequently assess beneficiary eligibility, ensuring resources are available for the millions of Americans who depend on Medicaid's safety net.

Strengthens and Protects the Medicare Program. The Budget proposes to reduce wasteful spending and incentivize efficiency and quality of healthcare in Medicare, extending the solvency of the program for America's seniors consistent with the President's promise to protect Medicare. The Budget brings transparency to several Medicare payments to hospitals, by financing payments not directly related to Medicare's health insurance role outside the Medicare Trust Fund and tying future growth to inflation growth; the Budget also reduces Medicare's spending on beneficiaries' unpaid cost sharing obligations, consistent with private sector business practices. In addition, the Budget proposes realigning incentives through site neutral payment reform to ensure accurate payments across different healthcare provider types are based on patient characteristics rather than site of care. By ensuring payments are accurately aligned with the costs of care and strengthening providers accountability to improve quality and health outcomes, the Budget protects seniors from excessive out-of-pocket costs and improves the standard of care they receive. The Budget also supports the Administration's commitment to reduce provider burden so providers can focus on patient care by eliminating reporting burden and low-value metrics in performance-based payment for physicians, improving incentives for physicians to participate in advanced payment models that reward high-value healthcare delivery, and providing CMS with greater flexibility in beneficiary education and quality assurance.

The Budget demonstrates the Administration's commitment to ensuring Medicare beneficiaries have access to timely and appropriate care, by reprioritizing primary care through a budget neutral increase to payments for primary care providers. The Budget proposes to expand seniors' personal control and introduce more consumer power into the healthcare market by allowing Medicare beneficiaries to make tax-deductible contributions to HSAs associated with high deductible health plans offered by their employers or Medicare Advantage plan. The Budget would extend Medicare's solvency by roughly eight years.

Supports Access to Innovative New Medical Technology. Consistent with the Administration's commitment to addressing barriers to healthcare innovation, the Budget includes several administrative actions and a legislative proposal aimed at ensuring Medicare beneficiaries have access to critical and life-saving new cures and other technologies that improve beneficiary health outcomes. In particular, the policies would instill greater transparency and consistency in how Medicare covers and pays for innovative technology. The Budget also proposes to test new ways of covering and paying for certain devices. For Medicare beneficiaries with diabetes, to improve health outcomes and cost savings for both beneficiaries and the Government, the Budget proposes expanding coverage of disposable devices that substitute for a durable device for use in the management and treatment of diabetes.

Launches an Initiative to End the HIV Epidemic in America. For more than three decades, the Nation and the world have confronted the challenges posed by HIV and AIDS. More than 700,000 Americans have lost their lives to HIV since 1987. Each year, there are approximately 40,000 new HIV infections in the United States, the majority clustered in a limited number of counties. For the first time in modern history, America has the ability to end the epidemic, with the availability of biomedical interventions such as antiretroviral therapy and pre-exposure prophylaxis (PrEP). This initiative is the first step toward this goal.

The Administration is proposing a new multiyear initiative focused on accelerating progress to eliminate new HIV infections in America, with the goal of reducing new infections by 75 percent within five years, and by 90 percent within 10 years. The 2020 Budget provides a total of $291 million to HHS for the Ending HIV Epidemic Initiative. Of this amount, the Budget provides $140 million for CDC to reduce new HIV infections by working closely with State and local health departments on intensive testing and referral to care efforts in areas of the Nation that constitute the majority of new infections. The Budget also includes $120 million for the Health Resources and Services Administration to deliver additional care and treatment for people living with HIV through the Ryan White HIV/AIDS Program and to supply testing, evaluation, prescription of PrEP, and associated medical costs for people who are at risk for HIV infections through the Health Centers program. In addition, the Budget prioritizes the reauthorization of the Ryan White program to ensure Federal funds are allocated to address the changing landscape of HIV across the United States. Reauthorization of the Ryan White Program should include data-driven programmatic changes as well as simplifying and standardizing certain requirements and definitions. These changes would ensure Federal funds may be allocated to populations experiencing high or increasing levels of HIV infections/diagnoses while continuing to support Americans already living with HIV across the Nation. The Indian Health Service would also receive funding to enhance HIV testing and linkages to care. In addition, the Initiative would leverage NIH current regional Centers for AIDS Research to refine implementation strategies to assure effectiveness of prevention and treatment.

Game-changing Progress on HIV Drugs

With advances in research and development, biomedical tools are now available to end the HIV epidemic in America. HIV antiretroviral therapy has progressed substantially from the drugs available in the 1990s. What were formerly multi-pill, high-toxicity regimens have progressed to more potent, one pill per day regimens with few side effects. In addition, there is now a groundbreaking single pill, pre-exposure prophylaxis (PrEP), which is proven to prevent HIV transmission. There are more than 1.2 million Americans at high risk for HIV for whom PrEP is indicated, yet only about 10 percent are currently on preventive therapy.

Reforms and Improves the U.S. Public Health Service Commissioned Corps (Corps). The Budget proposes to transform the Corps into a leaner and more efficient organization that would be better prepared to respond to public health emergencies and provide vital health services. The Budget significantly reduces the number of Corps officers working in non-mission critical positions and increases the number of officers working in mission critical positions. The Budget creates a Ready Reserve Corps similar to those used by other uniformed services to provide additional surge capacity during public health emergencies. The Budget also makes changes to the funding structure of the Corps' retirement pay and survivor's benefits to align with how the Government pays for almost all civilian and military retirement costs.

Prioritizes Critical Health Research. The Budget provides $33 billion to improve public health by advancing knowledge of living systems to tackle major health challenges and improve diagnosis, prevention, and treatment of diseases and disorders. With this investment, NIH would continue to address the opioid epidemic, make progress on developing a universal flu vaccine, and support the next generation of researchers. NIH has provided upfront funding for certain projects in recent years and would continue this approach in 2019 and 2020 to facilitate efficient management of NIH resources across multiple years. The Budget also supports cutting-edge intramural research by addressing the backlog of repair and improvement across NIH facilities. In addition, the Budget includes a new, dedicated effort to support research and develop new treatments for childhood cancer. Cancer is the leading cause of death from disease among children and adolescents in the United States. The basic biology of childhood cancers is not fully understood and differs from that of adult cancers. The Budget includes increased funding and an innovative initiative to enable the Nation's best researchers and doctors to learn from every child with cancer, providing the opportunity to comprehend finally the unique causes and the best cures for childhood cancer.

Strengthens Health Services for American Indians and Alaska Natives. The Budget expands access to direct health services for American Indians and Alaska Natives by funding the staffing and operations of new facilities and extending services to newly recognized Tribes. In addition, the Budget boosts recruitment and retention efforts for qualified health professionals by funding competitive employment packages for positions with high vacancies and building new staff quarters at remote sites. The Budget also begins a multiyear effort to modernize the Indian Health Service's electronic health record (EHR) system to promote interoperability between Federal health systems, as the Department of Veterans Affairs transitions to a new EHR system.

Enhances Emergency Preparedness and Health Security. Infectious disease outbreaks whether naturally occurring, such as an influenza pandemic, deliberate, or accidental, remain a serious threat to the U.S. homeland. HHS undertakes a variety of activities to prevent, mitigate, and respond to outbreaks and other public health threats. The Budget continues support for a variety of preparedness and response programs across HHS.

The Budget includes an increase of $10 million for the Strategic National Stockpile, compared to 2019 enacted, to enhance medical preparedness for chemical, biological, radiological, and nuclear threats. The Budget supports priority HHS biodefense and emergency preparedness such as the Biomedical Advanced Research and Development Authority, BioShield, and pandemic influenza. This funding would enable HHS to continue to build on investments to protect the civilian population in the event of public health emergencies related to infectious disease outbreaks, and other man-made crises.

As newly evolved strains of drug-resistant influenza viruses emerge that pose a significant threat to public health, as seen with the 2017 H7N9 avian influenza outbreak in China, the Budget continues to build on previous investments in pandemic preparedness and response capacity. Through the Assistant Secretary for Preparedness and Response and the Office of Global Affairs, the Budget provides $260 million to support investments in critical domestic influenza vaccine manufacturing facility infrastructure, continue the advanced research and development of improved vaccines, therapeutics, and rapid in-home diagnostics, and support international pandemic preparedness. The Budget also includes an increase of $10 million for CDC's influenza activities compared to 2019 enacted to support vaccine effectiveness studies, help expand the production capacity of cell-grown vaccine candidates, and undertake other high priority flu activities in support of the Administration's efforts to modernize influenza vaccines. The Budget also includes $50 million within CDC to build up the Infectious Diseases Rapid Response Reserve Fund. These funds provide needed flexibility for HHS agencies to quickly respond to emerging health threats as they arise.

The Budget includes $100 million to support CDC's global health security activities, an increase of $50 million compared to 2019 enacted. The Global Health Security Agenda is a multiyear global initiative to reduce infectious disease threats by strengthening the capacity of other countries to contain outbreaks at their source. Containing the spread of deadly infectious diseases through efficient biodefense capabilities is vital to protect the homeland and preserve U.S. national and economic security. CDC will implement a regional hub office model, allowing staff to more efficiently work in multiple countries in a region, as needed, to support health security priorities. CDC will primarily focus its activities on areas where it has seen the most success: lab and diagnostic capacity; surveillance systems; training of disease detectives; and establishing strong emergency operation centers.

Advances Medical Product Safety. The Budget provides $6.1 billion in total resources for FDA, $643 million more than the 2019 estimated level. The Budget includes $55 million to strengthen FDA's activities in response to the Nation's opioid crisis, $55 million to advance digital technology, $13.5 million for ensure that compounded drugs are safe and effective, and $20 million for a pilot program to develop and test technology that could detect pathogens in the blood supply.

Tackles the Epidemic of Youth E-Cigarette Use. The Budget includes a new user fee on e-cigarettes and other electronic nicotine delivery system products and proposes new FDA authority to collect user fees in support of its regulatory oversight of new tobacco and nicotine related products in the future as appropriate. The proposal would amend current law to add e-cigarette manufacturers and importers to a list of product categories subject to the user fee. The FDA's annual user fee cap of $712 million would be increased by $100 million and future collections of all tobacco related products would be indexed to inflation. This proposal would ensure that FDA has the resources to address today's alarming rise in youth e-cigarette use as well as new public health threats of tomorrow. New tobacco or nicotine products that are regulated by FDA should also pay a user fee, just as other tobacco related products that are subject to FDA's user fee.

Serves Older Americans. The Budget prioritizes funding for programs that address the needs of older Americans, many of whom require some level of assistance to continue living independently or semi-independently within their communities. This funding provides critical help and support to seniors, providing direct services such as respite care, transportation assistance, and personal care services. These services also include $907 million for senior nutrition programs. This funding is estimated to provide 221 million meals to more than 2.3 million older Americans nationwide.

Strengthens Work Requirements to Promote Self-Sufficiency. The Budget improves consistency between work requirements in federally funded public assistance programs, including Medicaid and Temporary Assistance for Needy Families (TANF), by requiring that able-bodied, working-age individuals find employment, train for work, or volunteer (community service) in order to receive welfare benefits. This would enhance service coordination for program participants, improve the financial well-being of those receiving assistance, and ensure federally funded public assistance programs are reserved for the most vulnerable populations.

Supports Children and Families in Achieving Their Potential. The Budget continues to invest in programs that help American families and children thrive. The Budget's investments in child care and early learning would help families access and afford the care they need while they work, go to school, or enroll in job training. The Budget maintains funding for Head Start and the Child Care and Development Block Grant at HHS. The Budget also proposes a $1 billion one-time mandatory investment for States to build the supply of care and stimulate employer investment in child care.

The Budget also supports States in providing key services to children and youth by increasing State flexibilities and reducing administrative burdens in foster care. These child welfare reforms focus on preventing the need for foster care unless absolutely necessary to ensure families can remain intact. In addition, the Budget promotes evidence-building and innovation to strengthen America's safety net, proposes improvements to the TANF program, and supports efforts to get noncustodial parents to work. Together, these proposals reflect the Administration's commitment to helping low-income families end dependency on Government benefits and promote the principle that gainful employment is the best pathway to financial self-sufficiency and family well-being.

Expands Statutory Access to the National Directory of New Hires (NDNH) for Program Integrity and Evidence Building. The Budget includes a package of proposals to provide valuable employment and earnings data—NDNH—for program integrity and evidence building activities, while ensuring privacy and security safeguards. Program integrity proposals to strengthen eligibility verification and/or reduce improper payments include those at HHS's CMS, the Railroad Retirement Board, and the Department of the Treasury's Do Not Pay Business Center on behalf of agencies with statutory access to NDNH. Evidence-building proposals include providing access for statistical agencies and evaluation offices, as well as access for State agencies to administer child support, workforce, and vocational rehabilitation programs. The package is detailed in *Analytical Perspectives*, Chapter 6, "Building and Using Evidence to Improve Government."

DEPARTMENT OF HOMELAND SECURITY

Funding Highlights:

- The Department of Homeland Security (DHS) protects Americans by safeguarding the homeland. The Department accomplishes its mission by: preventing terrorism; securing and managing the Nation's borders; administering and enforcing U.S. immigration laws; defending and securing Federal cyberspace; and ensuring disaster resilience, response, and recovery.
- The 2020 Budget prioritizes funding to secure the Nation's borders, strengthen and enforce U.S. immigration laws, and respond to and recover from major disasters and large-scale emergencies.
- High priority 2020 Budget investments include $5 billion for construction of the border wall, and $506 million to hire over 2,800 additional law enforcement officers and critical support personnel at U.S. Customs and Border Protection (CBP) and U.S. Immigration and Customs Enforcement (ICE). An additional $19.4 billion is available to help communities across the United States recover from the devastating impact of major disasters.
- The 2020 Budget requests $51.7 billion in discretionary appropriations for DHS, a $3.7 billion or 7.8-percent increase from the 2019 estimate (excluding 2019 amounts for Overseas Contingency Operations).

The President's 2020 Budget:

DHS protects Americans from threats by land, sea, air, and cyberspace, 24 hours a day, 365 days a year. The Department prioritizes smart, innovative, and effective programs to prevent terrorism, promote cybersecurity, manage America's borders, and enforce U.S. immigration laws, and it leads the Federal Government's coordinated and comprehensive Federal response to major disasters and other large-scale emergencies. The men and women of the Department work tirelessly to ensure the safety, preparedness, and resilience of the Nation. The Budget includes increased funding for border security, immigration enforcement, cybersecurity, and law enforcement capabilities. The Budget would allow the Department to adapt to new and evolving threats and challenges in order to protect the American people, the homeland, and U.S. values.

In addition to aggressively pursuing the resources necessary to support border security and immigration control, the Administration is calling upon the Congress to enact immigration reforms, including ending chain migration, canceling the visa lottery program, and moving from low-skilled migration to a merit-based immigration system, thereby raising wages, shrinking the deficit, and raising living standards for both U.S.-born and immigrant workers.

> *"Our policy at DHS in the face of growing dangers will not be 'strategic patience.' Instead, we are reasserting U.S. leadership. And we are building the toughest homeland security enterprise America has ever seen."*
>
> Kirstjen M. Nielsen
> Secretary
> September 5, 2018

Secures the Borders of the United States. Each day, DHS works to protect the American people and economy by preventing the illegal movement of people and contraband across U.S. borders while facilitating legitimate trade and travel to advance American prosperity. As depicted in the chart below, the number of people determined to be inadmissible at a port of entry or apprehended for illegally crossing the border grew by over 25 percent from 2017 to 2018, with illegitimate border crossers travelling as a family increasing by 53 percent.

Border security remains a top Administration priority, and the Budget continues to implement the President's direction to secure the U.S. Southwest border. The Budget requests $5 billion to construct approximately 200 miles of border wall along the U.S. Southwest border; provides $192 million to hire 750 Border Patrol agents, 171 CBP Officers, and support staff; and invests $367 million in CBP aircraft, vessels, surveillance technology, and equipment. In addition, the Budget includes $1.2 billion to continue to modernize U.S. Coast Guard vessels and aircraft that patrol and provide life-saving rescue missions across the Nation's coastal borders. The men and women of CBP work to keep the Nation safe from those seeking to smuggle people and contraband across America's borders. The Administration is pursuing innovative and effective solutions to hire and retain these valuable Government employees.

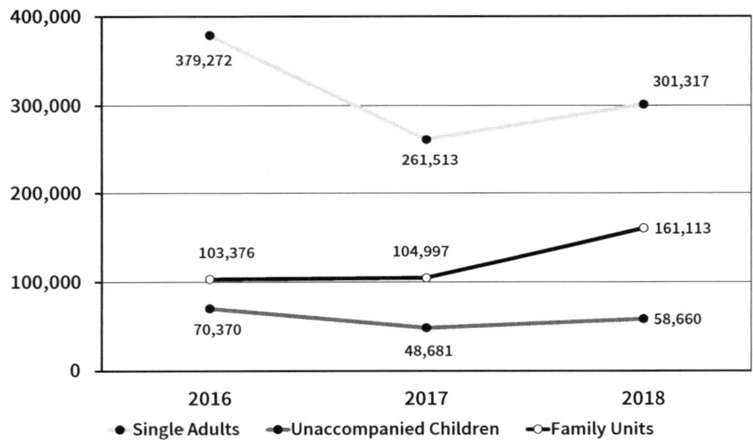

Source: Department of Homeland Security, 2018.

Enforces the Nation's Immigration Laws and Strengthens Border Security. The Budget provides discretionary and mandatory funding to promote the Administration's immigration and border security priorities and ensure the safety and security of American communities. While the Budget provides discretionary funding and investments to support a robust level of immigration and border security activities, these resources are insufficient to close existing loopholes in U.S. immigration laws and provide the full range of programs, activities, and staffing necessary. To bridge this gap, the Budget proposes the creation of a new Border Security and Immigration Enforcement Fund to be financed from mandatory receipts.

Provides Discretionary Funding to Support Enhanced Immigration and Border Security. The Budget provides $314 million to hire an additional 1,000 ICE law enforcement officers, 128 immigration court prosecuting attorneys, and 538 additional critical support staff to carry out this vital national security mission. Funding of $2.7 billion is provided for 54,000 detention beds to ensure ICE has the ability to detain criminal aliens and those apprehended at the border—including aliens with meritless asylum claims—so they can be safely removed. The Budget also makes additional investments in the Alternatives to Detention program for active monitoring of a total alien population of approximately 120,000. Moreover, the Budget increases funding for the Transportation and Removal programs to manage the growing numbers of family units and unaccompanied alien children apprehended at the border.

Provides Additional Mandatory Border and Immigration Enforcement Funding. The Administration proposes the creation of a Border Security and Immigration Enforcement Fund to provide the additional mandatory funding resources necessary to meet the President's border security and immigration enforcement goals. These goals include the expansion of immigration detention capacity to 60,000—including 10,000 family detention beds—and the hiring of 15,000 DHS law enforcement officers, 600 new ICE immigration court prosecuting attorneys, 100 new immigration judge teams and associated support at the Department of Justice's (DOJ) Executive Office for Immigration Review, and 50 new Federal prosecutors at DOJ's Offices of the United States Attorneys. The Administration plans to work with the Congress to identify offsets for these activities.

Reduces Illegal Immigration Work Incentives. The employment of illegal aliens by companies is a violation of the law, harms U.S. workers, and contributes to human smuggling, document fraud, identity theft, money laundering, and labor violations. The Budget proposes mandatory, nationwide use of the E-Verify system, an online tool that allows businesses to determine the eligibility of their employees to work in the United States. E-Verify is available at no cost to employers and has an accuracy rate of over 99.8 percent.[1] The Administration continues to require the use of E-Verify by Federal contractors to ensure the proper utilization of Federal dollars.

Secures U.S. Transportation Systems. The Transportation Security Administration (TSA) secures not just aviation, but also mass transit systems, passenger and freight railways, pipelines, highways, and ports. The Budget aggressively supports the deployment of new technologies, including 320 Computed Tomography units to the Nation's highest risk airports, and other new technologies to increase the effectiveness and efficiency of security operations for all modes of transportation. Approximately $7.8 billion is included in the Budget to support the TSA employees and technology that ensure the free movement of people and commerce.

Ensures Resilience to Disasters. The Budget provides significant investments for the Disaster Relief Fund to help affected communities that are continuing to recover from disasters in 2017 and 2018. The Budget proposes a $430 million all-hazards competitive grant program that would be rigorously evaluated to demonstrate how the Federal Emergency Management Agency is supporting communities to make the Nation safer and more resilient.

Flood insurance is the first line of defense for survivors to recover after flooding events. The Budget continues to hold the Administration's position that flood insurance rates should reflect the risk homeowners face by living in flood zones, while protecting low-income policyholders from rate increases they may otherwise face. The Administration is committed to the principle that homeowners share in the financial burden of protecting their property against the threat of flooding.

Supports the Cybersecurity of Government Networks and Critical Infrastructure. The President's National Cyber Strategy highlighted DHS's role in securing and building cybersecurity resilience for the Nation's most critical infrastructure, including Government networks. DHS works with key partners and stakeholders to identify and manage national cybersecurity risks. The Budget includes more than $1 billion for DHS's cybersecurity efforts. These resources would increase the number of DHS-led network risk assessments from 473 to 684—including assessments of State and local electoral systems—as well as for additional tools and services, such as the EINSTEIN and the Continuous Diagnostics and Mitigation programs, to reduce the cybersecurity risk to Federal information technology networks.

[1] *https://www.uscis.gov/e-verify/about-program/performance*

Addresses the Federal Cybersecurity Workforce Shortage. The *Delivering Government Solutions in the 21st Century* plan, released in June of 2018, included an initiative to solve the Federal cybersecurity workforce shortage by establishing a unified cyber workforce capability across the civilian enterprise. The Budget includes funding to support DHS's Cyber Talent Management System, which reflects the exemption of DHS's cyber workforce from many of the hiring and compensation requirements and restrictions in existing law under Title 5. Under this new initiative, DHS would hire at least 150 new cybersecurity employees using this system by the end of 2020. In this way, DHS would be better positioned to compete with the private sector for cyber talent.

Protects the Nation's Leaders by Strengthening the U.S. Secret Service. The Budget provides $2.3 billion for the U.S. Secret Service, fully supporting the Agency's dual missions of protecting the Nation's leaders while securing America's financial systems. The Budget proposes hiring an additional 177 special agents, officers, and professional staff at the U.S. Secret Service to continue to rightsize the Agency to perform its important missions. The Budget also provides funding for the 2020 presidential campaign and proposes investments in protective equipment and technology, consistent with recommendations of independent reviews of U.S. Secret Service operations.

DEPARTMENT OF HOUSING AND URBAN DEVELOPMENT

Funding Highlights:

- The Department of Housing and Urban Development (HUD) supports safe and affordable housing for Americans and provides access to homeownership opportunities.
- The Budget reflects the President's commitment to fiscal discipline by reforming programs to promote work and self-sufficiency, and focusing support on critical cost-effective programs that assist vulnerable households. The Budget also recognizes a greater role for State and local governments and the private sector.
- The Budget requests $44.1 billion in gross discretionary funding for HUD, an $8.7 billion or 16.4-percent decrease from the 2019 estimate.

The President's 2020 Budget:

HUD supports affordable housing for low-income families and provides access to homeownership for traditionally underserved first-time, low- and moderate-income, and minority homebuyers. The Budget provides $44.1 billion to support HUD's core functions. For HUD's rental assistance programs, the Budget provides $37.9 billion to maintain services to all currently assisted low-income families and proposes reforms that build on the Administration's Making Affordable Housing Work Act (MAHWA). This legislative proposal would not only reduce program costs, but also promote tenant work and self-sufficiency. In addition, the Budget continues to support efforts to remove lead and other hazards from housing, reduce homelessness, and make targeted investments in designated Opportunity Zones. For first-time and low- to moderate-income homebuyers, HUD's Federal Housing Administration (FHA) remains a critical source of mortgage financing. The Budget also provides critical resources for HUD's Financial Transformation Plan to address audit findings, ensure strong stewardship of taxpayer dollars, and increase transparency.

The Budget also redefines the proper role of the Federal Government by proposing to eliminate programs that have failed to demonstrate effectiveness, such as the Community Development Block Grant (CDBG) program, recognizing that State and local governments are better equipped to address local community and economic development needs.

Reforms Rental Assistance and Incorporates Uniform Work Requirements. The funding level for HUD's rental assistance programs provides sufficient resources to continue assistance to all 4.7 million currently served low-income families. To reduce the significant costs of these programs, the Budget re-proposes MAWHA and rent reforms that would require work-able individuals to shoulder more of their housing costs while providing an incentive to increase their earnings. Proposed rent reforms, however, would mitigate the impact on currently assisted elderly individuals and people with disabilities by phasing in a reduced rent increase over six years. The Administration's legislative proposal would also reduce administrative and regulatory burdens and allow communities further flexibility to develop rent requirements for tenants that are consistent with local needs and objectives.

In addition, the Budget incorporates the principles of the Administration's policy on uniform work requirements for non-elderly and non-disabled persons to work a minimum of 20 hours per week, or participate in training or educational activities. As a part of its implementation, HUD would explore ways to leverage existing compliance and enforcement mechanisms with the goal of avoiding additional burden on Public Housing Authorities and private multifamily property owners.

> *"The RAD program is a win-win. It preserves affordable housing for the people who need it most and transforms aging public housing into safer places to live..."*
>
> Brian Montgomery
> FHA Commissioner
> September 19, 2018

Leverages Capital for Housing Improvements. The Budget provides investments and statutory authorities to facilitate a shift from the Public Housing funding platform to Housing Vouchers and Project-Based Rental Assistance (PBRA). The Housing Voucher and PBRA programs benefit from leveraging both public and private financing to invest in long-term affordable housing stock. To advance this objective, the Budget requests $100 million for the Rental Assistance Demonstration (RAD) program, which supports the redevelopment of Public Housing units through conversion to Housing Voucher and PBRA units. Additional authorities in the Public Housing program, such as repositioning certain troubled public housing assets, would also assist in this effort. Recognizing this shift and that State and local governments should bear greater responsibility in providing affordable housing, the Budget does not request funding for the Public Housing Capital Fund.

Reduces Lead Exposure for Low-Income Children. Lead-based paint in housing presents one of the largest threats to the health, safety, and dreams of America's next generation, with more than 23 million homes having significant lead-based paint hazards. The Budget requests $290 million to promote healthy and lead-safe homes, $60 million above the 2019 estimated level. Research has shown that lead-based paint hazard control is an efficient and effective approach to reducing and preventing lead exposure, generating high returns on investments due to increased lifetime earnings and reduced medical costs. This funding level also includes resources for enforcement, education, and research activities to further support this goal.

Continues Supporting Communities' Efforts to Reduce Homelessness. The Budget provides $2.6 billion for the Homeless Assistance Grant (HAG) programs. HAG primarily funds the Continuum of Care (CoC) program, which is a coordinated community-based network of programs to prevent and address local homelessness. HUD awards CoC grants through a competitive funding process that promotes cost-effective and evidence-based strategies. As a part of the total, the Budget requests $270 million for Emergency Solutions Grants, which would enable municipalities to support emergency shelter, rapid re-housing, and homelessness prevention.

Promotes Economic Mobility and Improves Quality of Life. The Budget requests $75 million for the Family Self-Sufficiency program and $15 million for the Jobs-Plus Initiative. These programs connect HUD-assisted households to social services and employment resources, helping tenants maximize their earning potential and improve their financial situations and quality of life. A rigorous evaluation has shown that the Jobs-Plus Initiative produces lasting increases in tenant wages. The Secretary's EnVision Center research demonstration will also support this goal by providing communities centralized hubs that offer holistic approaches to self-sufficiency. In addition, the Budget requests funding for research and demonstrations to continue to build the evidence base for the most effective policies that promote economic self-sufficiency.

Targets Investments in Opportunity Zones. The Budget provides targeted resources aligned with the Administration's focus on encouraging investment in Opportunity Zones. The $100 million request for RAD, referenced above, would prioritize the redevelopment of Public Housing properties that are located in Opportunity Zones. The Budget also funds Technical Assistance to local municipalities that are seeking to attract public and private investments to their communities.

> *"...I've seen the negative impact lead exposure can have on a child's developing brain. HUD's Office of Lead Hazard Control and Healthy Homes has been a significant contributor to the ongoing development of a [F]ederal strategy to eliminate childhood lead poisoning, ensuring kids have a foundation and a home environment that contribute to their ability to thrive."*
>
> Ben Carson
> Secretary
> October 22, 2018

Supports Sustainable Homeownership Opportunities. The Budget preserves access to sustainable homeownership opportunities for creditworthy borrowers through FHA and Ginnie Mae credit guarantees. FHA provides a crucial source of mortgage financing for first-time homebuyers, who accounted for more than 80 percent of FHA-insured home purchase loans in 2018. The Budget requests $20 million above the 2019 estimated level to modernize FHA's outdated and burdensome information technology systems. This additional funding is fully offset by a modest new fee on FHA lenders, better aligning the responsibilities for the costs and benefits of this program. In addition, the Budget includes legislative proposals that would align FHA authorities with the needs of its lender enforcement program and limit FHA's exposure to down-payment assistance practices that not only increase the risk of taxpayer losses, but oftentimes are not in the best interest of borrowers.

Strengthens HUD's Financial Management. The Budget includes $20 million for HUD's Financial Transformation Plan, a multiyear effort to strengthen the agency's financial reporting, accounting operations and internal controls. This effort is critical to addressing recurring audit issues, ensuring strong stewardship of taxpayer dollars, and increasing transparency.

Eliminates Major Block Grants. The Administration continues to redefine the proper role of the Federal Government and proposes eliminating funding for programs that lack measurable outcomes or are ineffective. The Budget would eliminate several of HUD's community and economic development programs as well as affordable housing production programs. The Budget would eliminate CDBG, a program that has expended more than $150 billion since its inception in 1974, but has not demonstrated sufficient impact. Studies have shown that CDBG's allocation formula, which has not been updated since 1978, is ineffective at targeting funds to the areas of greatest need, and many aspects of the program have become outdated. The Budget would also eliminate the HOME Investment Partnerships Program, which has not been authorized since 1994. The Budget devolves responsibility to State and local governments, which are better positioned to assess local community needs and address unique market challenges.

DEPARTMENT OF THE INTERIOR

Funding Highlights:

- The Department of the Interior (DOI) conserves and manages natural resources and cultural heritage for the benefit and enjoyment of the American people, provides scientific and evidence-based information about America's natural resources and hazards, supports safe and responsible development of Federal energy resources, fosters rural prosperity, and honors the Nation's trust responsibilities and special commitments to American Indians, Alaska Natives, and U.S.-affiliated island communities to help them prosper.
- The 2020 Budget request for DOI prioritizes wildland fire risk mitigation, energy development programs, infrastructure improvements on public lands, and DOI-wide reorganization efforts. The Budget eliminates funding for unnecessary or duplicative programs while reducing funds for lower priority activities, including land acquisition and various grant programs.
- The Budget requests $12.5 billion for DOI, a $2 billion or 14-percent decrease from the 2019 estimate (including 2019 changes in mandatory programs).

The President's 2020 Budget:

DOI protects and manages the Nation's natural resources and cultural heritage, manages development of energy and mineral resources on Federal lands and waters, provides scientific and other information about the Nation's natural resources, manages water infrastructure, honors trust responsibilities to American Indians and Alaska Natives, and fulfills commitments to Insular areas. The 2020 Budget reflects the Administration's strong commitment to promoting economic security and energy dominance by developing domestic energy resources. These efforts invest in America's future and prioritize the safety and security of American taxpayers by reducing U.S. dependency on foreign nations.

Strengthens America's Energy Security. The Budget increases funding for DOI programs that support the safe and responsible development of energy on public lands and offshore waters. DOI has proposed an aggressive strategy for leasing offshore oil and gas under its Draft Proposed Program for 2019-2024. Onshore, the Administration is working aggressively to carry out congressional direction to implement oil and gas leasing in the coastal plain of the Arctic National Wildlife Refuge. The Department will also continue to make new areas available for renewable energy development—both onshore and offshore—and will prioritize renewable project permitting consistent with industry demand. The Budget also maintains funding for scientific research and data collection by the U.S. Geological Survey (USGS) to inform responsible energy and mineral development and minimize the environmental impacts of these activities. Combined with administrative reforms to streamline permitting processes, these efforts would provide industry with access to the energy resources America needs, while ensuring that taxpayers receive a fair return from the development of these public resources.

> *"Together, we are going to start a new energy revolution—one that celebrates American production on American soil."*
>
> President Donald J. Trump
> March 28, 2017

Supports Reorganization of DOI. The Budget provides $28 million to continue implementing DOI's vision for a reorganized Department, focusing resources on its new unified regions, moving headquarters staff west, and expanding the use of shared services. Through its 12 new unified regions, DOI hopes to improve collaboration and coordination across its bureaus on key DOI missions—such as recreation, conservation, and permitting—and to focus regions on the same resources and constituents. By relocating staff, the Department brings employees closer to the public that they serve and the resources they manage. Efforts to expand shared services will reduce duplicative capacity within DOI and increase the Department's ability to deliver on DOI's missions and responsibilities.

Supports Federal Efforts to Reduce Wildfire Risk. In light of historically catastrophic wildfire seasons in recent years, the Budget significantly increases funding for wildland fire management programs to reduce hazardous fuel loads and support wildfire preparedness efforts. The Budget responsibly funds base suppression costs pursuant to the Consolidated Appropriations Act, 2018, which would be bolstered by $300 million in additional suppression resources under the recently enacted wildfire cap adjustment. In addition, the Administration is unequivocal about the need to accelerate active forest management. The Budget reflects this critical priority by requesting $194 million for DOI's hazardous fuel mitigation work and $172 million for DOI timber programs; together, these programs help ensure that Federal lands and watersheds are sustainable, healthy, and productive. These programs also generate jobs in rural communities and help make them safer and more resilient to the destructive impacts of wildfire.

Invests in Public Lands Infrastructure Fund. DOI and the U.S. Department of Agriculture's Forest Service manage an infrastructure asset portfolio with a replacement value exceeding $300 billion. The buildings, trails, roads, water systems, and Bureau of Indian Education (BIE) schools managed by the Departments are deteriorating, as evidenced by a deferred maintenance backlog that exceeds $18 billion. To address this backlog, the Budget proposes a $6.5 billion Public Lands Infrastructure Fund (Fund) to improve and repair facilities at national parks and forests, wildlife refuges, BIE schools, and on other public lands. The Fund would be supported by the deposit of 50 percent of the proceeds received from Federal offshore and onshore energy leases over the 2020-2024 period, subject to an annual limit of $1.3 billion. These investments would improve some of America's most visited parks and public lands that support a multi-billion dollar outdoor recreation economy.

Preserves National Park Service (NPS) Assets for Future Generations. NPS has a long history of preserving and protecting the natural and cultural sites that tell America's story. To continue this tradition and ensure preservation of national parks for generations to come, the Budget provides $293 million to help address NPS's $12 billion deferred maintenance backlog. Along with the mandatory funding provided by the Public Lands Infrastructure Fund, this funding would help NPS maintain and preserve America's highest priority assets.

Prioritizes Land Management Operations at NPS, United States Fish and Wildlife Service, and Bureau of Land Management. To protect and conserve America's public lands, the Budget provides $5 billion for land management operations. These resources would ensure access to recreational activities such as hunting, fishing, and camping, and provide safe experiences for visitors. The Budget also advances efforts to streamline operations and reduce unnecessary spending.

Invests in Essential Science Programs. The Budget invests in USGS science related to natural hazards; water, energy, minerals, and other natural resources; and the health of America's ecosystems and environment. The Budget supports development of the Landsat 9 ground system, as well as research and data collection to inform sustainable energy and mineral development, responsible resource management, and natural hazard risk reduction.

Supports Tribal Sovereignty and Self-Determination across Indian Country. The Budget supports Federal trust responsibilities and tribal needs related to education, social services, law enforcement, infrastructure maintenance, and stewardship of land, water, and other natural resources. Funding priorities include core operational activities and services that support tribal sovereignty, sustain tribal governments, including assisting tribal law enforcement initiatives and training, and foster effective stewardship of trust resources, such as fully funding contract support costs. The Budget also supports BIE's efforts to foster the success of the approximately 47,000 students it serves.

Streamlines Reviews and Permitting. DOI is responsible for administering foundational environmental and historic preservation laws nationwide and for managing more than 20 percent of the Nation's lands, which affects the American public and many private stakeholders. The Budget supports DOI in fulfilling these important permitting and review responsibilities in a timely and thorough manner. As an example, the Budget maintains core funding for the United States Fish and Wildlife Service to conduct Endangered Species Act (ESA) consultations, which help facilitate development of infrastructure projects while ensuring threatened and endangered species receive the protections intended by the ESA. The Budget also strengthens the Bureau of Land Management's ability to efficiently facilitate and administer development of energy transmission projects.

Eliminates Unnecessary, Lower Priority, or Duplicative Programs. The Budget includes elimination of discretionary Abandoned Mine Land economic development grants that overlap with existing mandatory reclamation grants, National Heritage Areas that are more appropriately funded locally, Indian Guaranteed Loan Program funding that largely duplicates other existing loan programs serving Indian Country, and National Wildlife Refuge Fund payments to local governments that are duplicative of other payment programs.

Reduces Funding for Land Acquisition. The Budget continues to focus on using resources to manage existing lands and assets managed by DOI. For example, the Budget reduces funding for land acquisition to $8 million, including balance cancellations. Less funding for land acquisition would allow DOI to focus resources on supporting activities and asset repair in existing national parks, refuges, and public lands which encompass more than 500 million acres.

Supports Law Enforcement Capacity on Public and Trust Lands. DOI serves as the steward of more than 500 million acres of public lands and more than 55 million acres of tribal trust lands. The Budget keeps visitors and natural resources safe on the Nation's public lands and supports safe tribal communities on trust lands through law enforcement efforts. The Budget supports a strong and secure border, with DOI law enforcement efforts focused on the 12 million acres of DOI lands along the United States-Mexico border. The Budget also invests in the United States Park Police, who safeguard lives and protect America's national treasures. In addition, the Budget invests in efforts to combat illegal wildlife trafficking using United States Fish and Wildlife Service law enforcement capacity, in support of the President's Executive Order on combatting transnational criminal organizations.

Expands Recreational Access and Supports the Outdoor Recreation Economy. Each year, hundreds of millions of Americans visit U.S. national parks, wildlife refuges, and other public lands to hike, hunt, fish, view wildlife, and participate in other recreation opportunities. Visitors to public lands spend money in local gateway regions, and these expenditures generate and support economic prosperity within these local communities. In addition, through the purchases of hunting and fishing licenses and equipment—and associated excise taxes—sportsmen and women have generated billions of dollars to fuel wildlife and habitat conservation efforts. To serve these visitors, the Budget supports expanded public access to lands and waters administered by DOI. The Budget also invests in increased access to encourage sportsmen and women conservationists, veterans, minorities, and underserved communities that traditionally have low participation in outdoor recreation activities.

Invests in Water Resources and Infrastructure. The Budget invests in the safe, reliable, and efficient management of water resources throughout the United States. The Budget requests $1.1 billion for the Bureau of Reclamation, with an emphasis on operating, maintaining, and rehabilitating existing water resources infrastructure throughout the western United States. Through the Bureau of Reclamation and Bureau of Indian Affairs, the Budget requests $179 million for the implementation of enacted Indian water rights settlements in support of Federal trust responsibilities to Tribes. The Budget also invests $194 million in water-related science at USGS and the Bureau of Reclamation to sustain and enhance ground and surface water quality and quantity research and monitoring, and to develop new technologies to respond to the water resource challenges facing the Nation.

DEPARTMENT OF JUSTICE

Funding Highlights:

- The Department of Justice defends the interests of the United States and protects all Americans as the chief enforcer of Federal laws.
- The Budget prioritizes and protects investments in core Government functions such as national security, cybersecurity, violent crime reduction, immigration law, drug enforcement, and also addresses the opioid epidemic.
- The Budget requests $29.2 billion for the Department of Justice, a $698 million or 2-percent decrease from the 2019 estimate. The Budget targets funding increases to support public safety and national security while reducing or eliminating lower priority spending.

The President's 2020 Budget:

The Department of Justice enforces the laws and defends the interests of the United States; ensures public safety against foreign and domestic threats; provides Federal leadership in preventing and controlling crime; seeks just punishment for those guilty of crimes; and ensures the fair and impartial administration of justice for all Americans. After two consecutive years of increases in the violent crime rate, the estimated number of violent crimes in the Nation decreased 0.2 percent in 2017 when compared with 2016. The Department is committed to building on this success by expanding efforts to dismantle criminal networks, disrupt and prosecute human trafficking rings, halt the flow of illegal drugs, and restore law and order to communities. The Budget requests a total of $29.2 billion to expand the capacity of key law enforcement agencies and strengthen the Department's ability to address the most pressing public safety needs.

Enforces Immigration Laws. The Administration is committed to strengthening the Nation's security through robust enforcement of the Nation's immigration laws. Because of this increased enforcement, the Executive Office for Immigration Review (EOIR) received more than 230,000 new cases last year, bringing the pending caseload to over 750,000. To support this adjudicative need, the Budget provides a total of $673 million for EOIR, which includes funding to hire an additional 100 immigration judge teams and expand both physical and virtual courtroom space to conduct administrative immigration hearings.

Provides Additional Mandatory Border and Immigration Enforcement Funding. The Administration proposes the creation of a Border Security and Immigration Enforcement Fund to provide the additional mandatory funding resources necessary to meet the Administration's border security and immigration enforcement goals. These goals include the expansion of immigration detention capacity to 60,000—including 10,000 family detention beds—and the hiring of 15,000 Department of Homeland Security law enforcement officers, 600 new Immigration and Customs Enforcement immigration court prosecuting attorneys, 100 new immigration judge teams and associated support at EOIR, and 50 new Federal prosecutors at DOJ's Offices of the United States Attorneys. The Administration plans to work with the Congress to identify offsets for these activities.

Strengthens National Security. The Federal Bureau of Investigation (FBI) has responsibility for protecting U.S. citizens from harm both at home and abroad. In support of this vital work, the Budget provides $9.3 billion in Salaries and Expenses for the FBI. These resources would maintain and expand efforts across a wide array of important mission areas, including cybersecurity, transnational organized crime, and background checks for firearms purchases. In addition, the National Security Division is provided with $110 million, including resources to support additional work associated with the Foreign Investment Risk Review Modernization Act.

Calling for Bipartisan Action

"Our whole Nation benefits if former inmates are able to reenter society as productive, law-abiding citizens."

President Donald J. Trump
November 14, 2018

Supports Criminal Justice Reform. In addition to prosecuting crime and enforcing the Nation's laws, the Administration proposes to promote public safety by helping prevent individuals who have reentered society from returning to prison. Approximately 95 percent of incarcerated persons will eventually leave prison. However, individuals released from State prisons have a five-year recidivism rate of 77 percent, and those released from Federal prisons have a five-year recidivism rate of 42 percent. The Administration is committed to breaking this cycle of recidivism by better preparing individuals to reenter communities and to mitigating the collateral consequences of incarceration. In addition to backing criminal justice reform through the FIRST STEP Act, the Administration supports efforts to bolster evidence-based programming in Federal correctional institutions. The Budget provides approximately $754 million for reentry programming in the Bureau of Prisons, including funding for education, career and technical training, substance abuse, and residential reentry centers. Of this amount, the Budget provides $14 million for the development of new and innovative pilot programs designed to address the needs of individuals incarcerated in Federal prisons. In addition, through State and local assistance programs, the Budget provides $85 million for the Second Chance Act grant program to reduce recidivism and help returning citizens lead productive lives.

Combats Violent Crime. The Department of Justice is committed to restoring law and order by providing Federal resources where they are most needed and most effective. The Budget provides $14.9 billion for Federal law enforcement, including FBI, the Drug Enforcement Administration (DEA), the United States Marshals Service, the Bureau of Alcohol, Tobacco, Firearms, and Explosives (ATF), and the Organized Crime and Drug Enforcement Task Forces. These resources support the Department's ability to respond to national security crises; investigate violent and drug-related crime; and apprehend, detain, and prosecute offenders.

The Budget would transfer the entirety of the ATF alcohol and tobacco regulatory and enforcement responsibilities to the Alcohol and Tobacco Tax and Trade Bureau (TTB) in the Department of the Treasury. This transfer would enable ATF to hone its focus on activities that protect U.S. communities from violent criminals and criminal organizations, while consolidating duplicative alcohol and tobacco enforcement mechanisms within TTB. In addition, the operating capability of DEA's Special

Investigative Unit program would retain its critical role in enhancing the Federal Government's ability to pursue threat networks to their source, as prioritized in the National Security Strategy.

Tackles the Opioid Epidemic. Today, the United States faces the deadliest drug overdose crisis in American history. More than 70,000 Americans lost their lives to drug overdoses in 2017. Evidence shows that fentanyl, heroin, or prescription opioids were responsible for nearly 48,000 of these tragic deaths. The Department of Justice recognizes its critical role in combating prescription opioid misuse and illicit heroin and fentanyl use. The Budget provides $2.3 billion in discretionary resources for DEA, including an additional $35 million to enhance heroin enforcement efforts, end anonymous online drug trafficking, and pursue transnational criminal organizations profiting from these deadly substances. The Budget also provides $443 million in fee-funded resources for DEA's Diversion Control Fee Account to combat the diversion of licit drugs and precursor chemicals. These efforts are bolstered by an additional $4 million to deploy 23 United States Attorney opioid prosecutors to districts hardest hit by this crisis. In addition, the Budget includes $330 million for opioid-related State and local assistance including: $145 million for the Comprehensive Opioid Abuse Program to support treatment and recovery, diversion, and alternatives to incarceration programs; $125 million for Drug Courts, Mental Health Courts, and Veterans Treatment Courts; $30 million for Residential Substance Abuse Treatment; and $30 million for Prescription Drug Monitoring Programs.

Supports State and Local Law Enforcement. The Budget also supports key State and local assistance programs, including $405 million for the Byrne Justice Assistance Grants Program, which provides State and local governments with crucial Federal funding to prevent and control crime. In addition, the Budget provides $100 million for the Violent Gang and Gun Crime Reduction/Project Safe Neighborhoods (PSN) program. PSN creates safer communities through sustained reductions in gang violence and gun crime by leveraging Federal, State, and local partnerships. The Budget further reflects the Administration's commitment to keeping children safe by providing $100 million in STOP School Violence Act funding. This critical program supports a variety of school safety programs including training for school personnel, preventative tip lines and threat assessments, and coordination between schools and law enforcement. In addition, the Budget supports critical victim assistance programs, including $492 million in Violence Against Women Act funding and $77 million to support victims of human trafficking.

Protecting America's Children

"Through the STOP School Violence grants, we are giving local schools and police departments the resources they need to hire more officers, and train more teachers, and better detect and address early warning signs of mental illness before it's too late."

President Donald J. Trump
October 8, 2018

DEPARTMENT OF LABOR

Funding Highlights:

- The Department of Labor (DOL) supports the Nation's wage earners, job seekers, and retirees.
- The Budget focuses DOL on its highest priority functions and restores fiscal discipline by eliminating programs that are duplicative, unnecessary, unproven, or ineffective. The Budget also takes steps to reorganize and modernize the Agency's operations so taxpayer dollars are spent efficiently.
- The Budget requests $10.9 billion for DOL, a $1.2 billion or 9.7-percent decrease from the 2019 enacted level.

The President's 2020 Budget:

DOL supports American workers, job seekers, and retirees by providing resources and opportunities to improve their skills, find work, and enter or return to the workforce. The Department also safeguards their working conditions, health and retirement benefits, and wages. Workers are the backbone of the American economy, and the Nation needs a skilled and productive workforce to keep the economy growing. The Budget improves the quality of life for all workers by making targeted, evidence-based investments to help workers remain competitive in the workforce and by eliminating duplicative, wasteful, and non-essential activities.

Builds a Highly Skilled and Competitive Workforce

Expands Access to Apprenticeship. The Budget invests $160 million in apprenticeship, a proven earn-while-you-learn strategy that equips workers with the skills they need to fill open, high-paying jobs. The Budget also proposes to increase H-1B fee revenues in order to fund additional apprenticeship activities. Apprenticeship is a great solution for employers looking for a skilled workforce and workers looking for an affordable path to a secure future. As part of implementing the President's Executive Order "Expanding Apprenticeships in America," the Department is establishing a new industry-recognized apprenticeship system to modernize and expand the U.S. approach to apprenticeships. In 2018, there were 238,549 new apprentices, a 20-year high. DOL is working to further expand apprenticeships by empowering third party "accreditors" to recognize new, industry-driven apprenticeship programs, focusing on those in high-growth sectors where apprenticeships are underutilized, such as healthcare, information technology, and advanced manufacturing.

Closes the Skills Gap by Training American Workers. The Budget proposes to double the American Competitiveness and Workforce Improvement Act of 1998, as amended, fee for the H-1B visa program to prepare American workers for jobs that are currently being filled by foreign workers, especially in science, technology, engineering, and mathematics fields. The increased revenue would support DOL's grants to expand apprenticeship and provide additional support for technical skills instruction at the K-12 and community college levels through the Department of Education's Career and Technical Education formula grants.

Moves toward Reorganizing and Consolidating the Nation's Workforce Development Programs. Currently, the Federal Government has more than 40 workforce development programs spread across 15 agencies with a total annual cost of approximately $18 billion. In its *Delivering Government Solutions in the 21st Century* plan, the Administration proposed Government-wide workforce development program consolidation, streamlining separate programs in order to increase efficiencies and better serve American workers. The Administration looks forward to working with the Congress to achieve this necessary restructuring, and the Budget takes steps in this direction by eliminating programs that are ineffective, unproven, or duplicative.

> *"[W]e recognize the importance of apprenticeships in helping our country's hardworking people develop the competencies that enable success in today's dynamic, 21st [C]entury economy."*
>
> President Donald J. Trump
> November 9, 2018

Supports America's Veterans. The Budget invests in the Nation's veterans, transitioning servicemembers, and their spouses by better assisting their transitions from active duty to civilian life. The Budget increases funding for the Transition Assistance Program to assist servicemembers in their transition to civilian employment. The Budget also provides funding to support military spouses, who are often required to find new opportunities after their spouse has been relocated. In addition, the Budget provides funding for the Veterans Employment and Training Services' core programs, which help improve skills and provide employment opportunities for veterans across the United States.

Reforms Job Corps. Job Corps educates and provides skills instruction to approximately 50,000 disadvantaged youth at 123 primarily residential centers across the United States. The Budget takes aggressive steps to improve Job Corps for the youth it serves by: improving center safety; empowering new, more effective entities to operate centers; focusing the program on the older youth for whom the program is more effective; and closing centers that inadequately prepare students for jobs. As part of this reform effort, the Budget ends the Department of Agriculture's (USDA) role in the program, unifying responsibility in DOL. Workforce development is not a core USDA role, and the 25 centers it operates are overrepresented in the lowest performing cohort of centers. The Budget also proposes new legislative flexibilities that would enable the Department to more expediently close low-performing centers, target the program to groups more likely to benefit, and make the necessary capital investments to ensure successful pilot programs. These reforms would save money and improve results by eliminating ineffective centers and finding better ways to educate and provide skills instruction to youth.

Improves the Delivery of America's Economic Statistics. The Budget recognizes the importance of economic statistics for businesses and everyday citizens to make informed decisions and confidently invest in America's future. The Administration urges the Congress to favorably consider the *Delivering Government Solutions in the 21st Century* plan's recommendation to consolidate within the Department of Commerce critical economic statistics programs at the Census Bureau, the Bureau of Economic Analysis, and the Bureau of Labor Statistics, making agency operations more efficient, improving products, and reducing the burden on respondents, while preserving the Agencies' brand recognition and independence.

Modernizes the Unemployment Safety Net to Emphasize Work

Combats Waste, Fraud, and Abuse in the Unemployment Insurance Program. The Federal-State Unemployment Insurance (UI) program has continually had one of the highest rates of improper payments in the Federal Government. More than 13 percent of the program's payments, representing $3.7 billion, are paid to individuals that do not meet all of the program's eligibility requirements. The Budget takes aggressive steps to address this problem by providing grants to States to combat the top two root causes of improper payments in their programs. The Budget also reduces waste, fraud, and abuse in the UI program with a package of program integrity proposals. These proposals to combat improper payments are based on tools that States already have at their disposal but would require that States use those tools to spend certain UI program funds on activities that reduce waste, fraud, and abuse in the system. The Budget also supports the UI Integrity Center of Excellence, which is developing a data hub to allow States to access a fraud analytics database to identify fraud as effectively as possible.

Focuses Trade Adjustment Assistance on Apprenticeship and Other Work-Based Training. The Trade Adjustment Assistance (TAA) program, which provides cash benefits and training to workers who have been displaced as a result of international trade, is in need of reform. A rigorous 2012 evaluation of the program demonstrated that workers who participated in the program had lower earnings than the comparison group at the end of a four-year follow-up period,[1] in part because they were more likely to participate in long-term job training programs rather than immediately reentering the workforce. However, this training was not targeted to in-demand industries and occupations—only 37 percent of participants became employed in the occupations for which they trained. The Budget proposes to refocus the TAA program on apprenticeship and on-the-job training, earn-as-you-learn strategies that ensure that participants are training for relevant occupations in today's competitive workforce. States would also be encouraged to place a greater emphasis on intensive reemployment services for workers who are not participating in work-based training, getting those workers back into the workforce more quickly.

Protects American Workers

Makes Health Insurance More Affordable for Small Businesses. The President's Executive Order "Promoting Healthcare Choice and Competition Across the United States" directed the Secretary of Labor to consider expanding access to health coverage by allowing more employers to form Association Health Plans (AHPs), arrangements under which small businesses may band together to offer competitive and affordable health insurance to their employees. The Budget supports this initiative by increasing funding for the Employee Benefits Security Administration to develop policy, regulations, and enforcement capacity to enable more employers to adopt the AHP model and expand health insurance access for American workers.

Secures Safe and Healthy Workplaces. The Budget maintains targeted investments in the Occupational Safety and Health Administration (OSHA) and Mine Safety and Health Administration (MSHA) aimed at preventing worker fatalities, injuries, and illnesses through enforcement, outreach, and compliance assistance. The Budget includes funding for additional OSHA inspectors to conduct more inspections in high-hazard industries and for protecting whistleblowers' rights. The Budget proposes a new budget activity within MSHA, consolidating the Coal Mine Safety and Health and the Metal and Nonmetal Mine Safety and Health budget activities. The new enforcement structure would provide the flexibility to address industry changes and maximize the efficient use of MSHA's resources.

---

1 *https://www.mathematica-mpr.com/our-publications-and-findings/publications/the-evaluation-of-the-trade-adjustment-assistance-program-a-synthesis-of-major-findings*

Rebuilds DOL's Role in Overseeing Union Integrity. To help safeguard labor union democracy and financial integrity, the Budget takes steps to restore the Office of Labor-Management Standards' investigative workforce, which has fallen by more than 40 percent during the past 10 years. The Budget would strengthen protections for union members by supporting more audits and investigations to uncover flawed officer elections, fraud, and embezzlement.

Protects Americans' Pensions. The Pension Benefit Guaranty Corporation's (PBGC) multiemployer program, which insures the pension benefits of 10 million workers, is at risk of insolvency by 2025. As an important step to protect the pensions of these hardworking Americans, the Budget proposes to add new premiums to the multiemployer program, raising approximately $18 billion in premiums over the 10-year window. At this level of premium receipts, the program is projected to remain solvent over the next 20 years, helping to ensure that there is a safety net available to workers and retirees whose multiemployer plans fail. The Budget proposes to rebalance premiums in the single-employer program, which insures pension plans that are maintained by individual employers. The Budget proposes to freeze for one year premium rates for well-funded plans, which have faced numerous premium increases since 2012, and shift the premium burden to underfunded plans that pose a greater solvency risk to PBGC.

Reforms the Federal Employees' Compensation Act. The Budget proposes to reform the Federal Employees' Compensation Act program, which provides workers' compensation benefits to Federal employees injured or killed on the job and their survivors. The proposed reforms would save taxpayer dollars by modernizing program administration, simplifying benefit rates, and introducing controls to prevent waste, fraud, and abuse.

Puts American Workers First. DOL administers the labor certification component of foreign temporary work visa programs, which ensure that American workers are not unfairly displaced or disadvantaged by foreign workers. The certification programs lack a reliable workload-based source of funding, which has created recurring seasonal backlogs for employers. The Budget proposes to establish fees to create a workload-based funding source and place responsibility for funding this work on the program's users rather than taxpayers.

Supports Working Families

Provides for Paid Family Leave for New Parents. The Budget invests in a better future for Americans with a proposal to provide paid family leave to new mothers and fathers, including adoptive parents, so all families can afford to take time to recover from childbirth and bond with a new child. The proposal would allow States to establish paid parental leave programs in a way that is most appropriate for their workforce and economy. The Administration looks forward to working with the Congress to advance policies that would make paid parental leave a reality for families across the Nation.

Makes Government More Efficient

Tackles Duplication and Inefficiency at DOL. DOL is acting to implement in-house reforms consistent with the President's directive to reorganize and improve the Federal Government. Many of DOL's administrative activities, including information technology, procurement, human resources, financial management, and physical security, are separated across its subcomponents. This creates duplication, limits economies

> *"Paid family leave enables parents to balance the competing demands of work and family, pursue their careers, and build strong and thriving families. It is an investment in the future of our workers, our families, and our country."*
>
> Ivanka Trump
> Advisor to the President
> July 11, 2018

of scale, and prevents resources from being spent on core mission-related work. DOL is working to centralize these activities to improve oversight, eliminate duplication, save money, and achieve economies of scale. In addition, the Budget includes funding and more flexibilities for DOL's Chief Information Officer to modernize the Department's legacy case management systems by reallocating base resources.

DEPARTMENT OF STATE AND OTHER INTERNATIONAL PROGRAMS

Funding Highlights:

- The Department of State, the U.S. Agency for International Development (USAID), and other international programs promote the national security and economic prosperity of the United States by advancing diplomacy, security, and fair economic competition.
- The Budget for the United States' international programs advances the Nation's strategic objectives, including those outlined in the National Security Strategy of the United States. The Budget supports new tools to allow the United States to respond flexibly to international challenges, as well as organizational reforms to increase agency effectiveness. These reforms prioritize the efficient use of taxpayer dollars and increased burden-sharing to rebalance U.S. contributions to international organizations.
- The Budget requests $40.0 billion for the Department of State and USAID, a $12.3 billion or 23-percent decrease from the 2019 estimate. The Budget also requests $1.6 billion for Department of the Treasury international programs, approximately equal to the 2019 estimate.

The President's 2020 Budget:

The President's Budget supports the Department of State, USAID, and other international programs to protect U.S. citizens, increase American prosperity, and advance the development of democratic societies. The Budget provides the necessary resources for the United States to expand its influence and safeguard its economic interests, even as competition from rising powers increases. To achieve this, the Budget invests in new capabilities to defend American interests and values across the security, trade, and information domains. The Budget supports America's reliable allies, but reflects a new approach toward countries that have taken unfair advantage of the United States' generosity. The Budget restores fiscal discipline by eliminating ineffective programs and initiating wide-reaching agency reforms. The Budget also recalibrates American contributions to international organizations to a more sustainable level, maintaining American leadership while asking other nations to increase participation. Through the strategic, efficient use of resources, the Budget would reduce spending while adapting U.S. international agencies to the current era and providing better results for the American people.

Supports More Effective American Diplomacy

Supports the U.S. Diplomatic Presence to Advance America's Interests and Protect National Security. The Budget requests $4.7 billion for diplomatic programs supporting

Department of State professionals working every day to achieve U.S. foreign policy objectives and advance American interests through a network of 277 embassies, consulates, and diplomatic missions around the world. This funding level sustains and invests in the State Department's workforce, allowing the Department to recruit and develop its personnel to meet high priority needs while promoting efficient operations. The Budget would enable the Department to continue modernizing its information technology platform to allow its workforce to do their jobs efficiently, effectively, and securely. In addition, the Budget includes $3.8 billion for consular and border security programs, financed through fee collections, to carry out passport and visa functions. This critical component of U.S. border security protects the American people while facilitating legitimate travel. The Budget also requests $1.3 billion for USAID operating expenses to support USAID personnel in 87 missions.

Prioritizes Embassy Security to Protect Diplomats and Staff. The Budget requests $4.7 billion to protect overseas personnel and facilities, including the Department's share of the $2.2 billion requested Government-wide for new, secure embassy construction, as recommended by the Benghazi Accountability Review Board. This security funding supports the protection of every U.S. diplomatic mission and the thousands of employees who serve U.S. interests overseas in dangerous and challenging security environments. With the proposed level of funding, the Department of State would continue to protect American personnel representing more than 30 agencies, as well as provide services to Americans overseas, in a safe and secure environment.

Supports Strategic Partners and Diplomatic Progress. The Budget fully supports the U.S.-Israel Memorandum of Understanding and includes $3.3 billion in Foreign Military Financing grant assistance to bolster Israel's capacity to defend itself against threats in the region and maintain its qualitative military edge. The Budget also fully supports the U.S.-Jordan Memorandum of Understanding and the U.S. diplomatic and security partnership with Egypt. The Budget includes a Diplomatic Progress Fund, which would allow the United States to incentivize and take advantage of diplomatic openings and opportunities to advance the Nation's foreign policy priorities as they arise. This Fund provides flexibility to respond to improved engagement from governments for which the Budget has not proposed specific bilateral funding, such as non-security assistance for the West Bank and Gaza, should diplomatic progress be achieved in support of U.S. objectives and regional peace. The Administration continues to assess how best to advance regional peace and stability, counter destabilizing activities and influence, and ensure resources are appropriately aligned with U.S. national security and economic interests. The Budget also continues robust assistance to support religious and ethnic minorities across the Middle East and elsewhere.

Supports a Peaceful Resolution to the Afghan Conflict. The Budget provides $533 million for assistance to Afghanistan. The Budget prioritizes economic growth and reconciliation, investments to help Afghanistan to work toward peace. The Budget supports programs that target private-sector led economic growth, including by increasing the country's export capability and attracting international investment. The Budget also supports education, health, governance, and other sectors that are necessary for a stable and thriving Afghanistan.

Emphasizes Great Power Competition

Advances a Free and Open Indo-Pacific. The Nation's future security, prosperity, and leadership depends on maintaining a free and open Indo-Pacific region. The Budget provides over $1 billion for the Indo-Pacific, reflecting the Administration's commitment to the region. This funding supports democracy and good economic governance, private sector mobilization and competitiveness, critical infrastructure standards and financing, and security cooperation. The new Development Finance Corporation's (DFC) work in the region will also advance U.S. strategy by leveraging private sector capital in much needed, high-quality regional infrastructure. Together, these programs ensure that the United States remains the preferred security and economic partner in the region.

Counters Russian Malign Influence. The Budget provides over $500 million for assistance to Europe, Eurasia, and Central Asia to: advance shared security; safeguard the territorial integrity of U.S. allies; support partner countries' efforts to transition away from Russian military equipment, particularly through Foreign Military Finance lending; and address weaknesses in the macro-economic environment that the Government of Russia seeks to exploit, such as dependence on energy and trade.

> *"We believe that when nations respect the rights of their neighbors, and defend the interests of their people, they can better work together to secure the blessings of safety, prosperity, and peace."*
>
> President Donald J. Trump
> September 25, 2018

Advances Fair and Reciprocal Trade. The Budget increases funding for the Office of the U.S. Trade Representative (USTR) in support of the President's trade agenda. The Administration has renegotiated outdated agreements with Canada, Mexico, and South Korea, and is pursuing new agreements with the European Union, Japan, and the United Kingdom. These efforts will help ensure that fair trade grows the economy and supports jobs at home. The Administration further protects American workers and businesses by identifying trade violations and pursuing enforcement options to end abuses. Robust support for USTR would also help support implementation of the Foreign Investment Risk Review Modernization Act, which helps protect U.S. businesses and technology from intellectual property theft.

Supports Fair Competition for American Exporters. The Budget supports a fully functioning Export-Import Bank (ExIm) to implement reforms and help American exporters compete in an increasingly unfair global marketplace. The Budget ensures ExIm would be able to help correct market failures, especially by supporting small businesses, sectors with national security importance, and American companies with foreign-government supported competitors.

Makes Programs More Effective While Increasing Burden Sharing

Maintains U.S. Global Humanitarian Leadership while Expecting Others to Do More. The Budget requests significant humanitarian assistance resources that would enable the United States to remain the largest single humanitarian donor in the world. These resources would address major humanitarian crises, including those driven by conflict, such as in Syria, Yemen, and Iraq. The Budget continues the new approach to relief announced in the 2019 Budget to influence other donors to give a greater funding share and to demand improved performance by United Nations (UN) and other implementers in order to maximize benefits for recipients. The new approach strives for greater accountability by international partners along with donor burden sharing that is more balanced, while reducing suffering and meeting the needs of refugees and displaced persons close to their homes until they can return safely. As conflict-based crises increase and force multiple displacements of populations within and outside their national borders, the Budget proposes to adapt and significantly improve America's ability to respond flexibly by consolidating all overseas humanitarian assistance in a single account so that funds can adjust as needed to reach affected persons. U.S. refugee admissions will continue to be funded through the Migration and Refugee Assistance account, a separate State Department account.

Pushes Multilateral Organizations Toward Fairer Burden Sharing and Advancing U.S. Interests. The Budget supports the aims of the National Security Strategy that the United States will "compete and lead in multilateral organizations so that American interests and principles are protected" and therefore "will prioritize [our] efforts in those organizations that serve American interests..." but "where existing institutions and rules need modernizing, the United States will lead to update them." In line with these objectives, the Budget prioritizes U. S. contributions to organizations that most closely align with American interests. The Administration continues to seek greater transparency and reform across the multilateral sphere, including by strategically assessing United Nations peacekeeping missions and demanding increased efficiency and effectiveness from all international organizations, while also seeking a more equitable distribution of financial responsibility.

Maintains U.S. Leadership at Multilateral Development Banks (MDBs). The Budget requests $1.6 billion in funding for MDBs, including a new commitment for the World Bank's International Bank for Reconstruction and Development where the United States remains the largest shareholder. As a leading donor, the United States demands financial discipline, high performance and accountability, fair burden sharing, and strategic investments that serve U.S. development, foreign policy, and national security goals.

Continues U.S. Leadership Against HIV/AIDS, and Mobilizes Others to Contribute More. For the next replenishment of the Global Fund to Fight AIDS, Tuberculosis and Malaria, the Budget offers to match $1 for every $3 pledged by other donors, providing a $1.1 billion contribution in 2020 and up to $3.3 billion over the three-year replenishment period, using unmatched funds appropriated by the Congress for 2019 from the last replenishment. This new match will support a global target of $13.2 billion, an increase from the previous replenishment, and challenges other donors to make significant new commitments to fighting the three diseases. The Budget also provides $3.4 billion for the U.S. President's Emergency Plan for AIDS Relief (PEPFAR), fully funding the final year of the Administration's *Strategy for Accelerating HIV/AIDS Epidemic Control (2017-2020)*, when coupled with additional resources appropriated by the Congress in 2019. With these resources, PEPFAR would provide lifesaving support in more than 50 countries, maintain all current patients on treatment, and continue the United States' position as the world's top HIV/AIDS donor.

Protects the United States and the World From Infectious Disease Through the Global Health Security Agenda (GHSA). To prevent, detect, and respond to infectious disease threats before they reach U.S. borders, the Budget continues significant support through a renewed commitment for the next five-year phase of GHSA. This commitment would bolster an international partnership to reduce the likelihood of outbreaks abroad and strengthen the capacity of countries to respond. The Budget also requests more than $2 billion for lifesaving programs to address maternal and child health, family planning, nutrition, malaria, neglected tropical diseases, and for the U.S. contribution to Gavi, the Vaccine Alliance. The Budget prioritizes resources to combat tuberculosis, the most lethal infectious disease in the world, with an emphasis on drug-resistant tuberculosis through a new business model that promotes sustainable partnerships with local organizations.

Reorganization and Reform: Supports New Tools and Needed Reforms

Strengthens U.S. Allies and Bilateral Security Relationships by Helping Partner Countries Buy More U.S. Defense Articles and Services. The Budget proposes to expand the U.S. Government's toolkit for financing U.S. defense sales by requesting expanded authority to provide Foreign Military Financing (FMF) loans. New for 2020, the Budget requests interest rate flexibility for the FMF direct loan program to make U.S. defense equipment a more competitive and more affordable option for partner countries. The Budget also requests authority to provide partial U.S. Government-backed loan guarantees to incentivize the private sector to fill the defense financing gap, reducing the risk to U.S. taxpayers. This reformed FMF loan program would serve to complement the Budget's request for $5.4 billion in FMF grant assistance so that America can still be the defense supplier of choice for partner countries for which loans are not the best option. This expanded set of

FMF tools would help support increased U.S. defense sales and increase opportunities for allies and partners to build their militaries around U.S. innovation and quality.

Implements New Development Finance Legislation to Increase U.S. Influence. On October 5, 2018, the President signed into law the Better Utilization of Investments Leading to Development Act. The legislation consolidates, modernizes, and reforms the U.S. Government's "development finance" capabilities—primarily, the Overseas Private Investment Corporation and USAID's Development Credit Authority—into the U.S. International DFC, consistent with the Administration's *Delivering Government Solutions in the 21st Century* reform plan. For its first year in operation, the Budget provides $300 million to the DFC for its operations and to extend loans, guarantees, and political risk insurance. This amount also supports a new equity investment program and other support to facilitate private-sector investment in emerging markets that would have positive developmental impact. These are transactions that the private sector will not undertake on its own. These tools would allow the U.S. Government to better partner with allies and deliver financially-sound alternatives to state-led initiatives from countries like China.

Optimizes Fragmented and Outdated Humanitarian Assistance Structure. In its *Delivering Government Solutions in the 21st Century* reform plan, the Administration committed to make fundamental changes to optimize the effectiveness of the Nation's fragmented and outdated humanitarian assistance structure. In addition to the previously-announced merger of USAID's humanitarian offices, the Budget consolidates the overseas humanitarian assistance programming currently conducted by the Department of State into the new bureau at USAID. In addition, all humanitarian assistance would be funded through a single, flexible appropriations account. This reorganization builds on each organization's comparative advantages by leveraging USAID's program implementation and partner oversight expertise with the State Department's expertise on humanitarian policy, diplomacy, and refugee issues. The Budget pairs this restructuring with a high-level, dual-hat humanitarian leadership structure at the Department of State and USAID under the authority of the Secretary of State. The Department of State would continue management and implementation of the U.S. Refugee Admissions Program through the Migration and Refugee Assistance account. This restructuring and consolidation would facilitate dynamic funding allocations and program coordination across refugees abroad, those displaced within their own country, and other victims as conflict-driven crises evolve. This restructuring is critical to establishing a strong, unified U.S. voice that can extract optimal UN reforms and deliver long-overdue optimal outcomes for beneficiaries and taxpayer dollars.

Transforms USAID and Promotes Self-Reliance. The Budget reflects the Administration's goal of reducing the long-term need for foreign assistance by helping partner countries become self-reliant. The Budget prioritizes investments in private-sector led growth, domestic resource mobilization, and economic and governance reforms, informed by objective metrics and roadmaps that track progress and identify areas for emphasis. These programs aim to catalyze sustainable economic growth in recipient countries, and to allow countries to solve their own development challenges. The recently launched Women's Global Development and Prosperity Initiative represents the type of responsible spending the Administration seeks to achieve, through establishing a cohesive whole-of-government approach to women's economic empowerment, tracking rigorous metrics, and leveraging partners' resources to achieve shared goals. In addition, the Budget supports implementation of the comprehensive set of reforms outlined in the Administration's *Delivering Government Solutions in the 21st Century* reform plan, including a major structural reorganization of USAID to strengthen core capabilities, increase efficiency, and reduce costs. This also includes the creation of a small grants office that would consolidate the African Development Foundation and the Inter-American Foundation into USAID, thus elevating the small-grants function as a tool of development and diplomacy and sharing best practices with USAID.

DEPARTMENT OF TRANSPORTATION

Funding Highlights:

- The mission of the Department of Transportation (DOT) is to ensure that the Nation has the safest, most efficient and modern transportation system in the world; the system improves the quality of life for all American people and communities, from rural to urban; and the system increases the productivity and competitiveness of American workers and businesses.
- The Budget request for DOT focuses on its critical transportation safety mission and provides targeted investments in competitive programs that effectively leverage Federal resources to spur larger, partnership-driven investment in infrastructure in key areas.
- The Budget requests $21.4 billion in discretionary budget authority for 2020, a $5.9 billion or 22-percent decrease from the 2019 discretionary estimate. The Budget also provides $62.2 billion in mandatory funds and obligation limitations.

The President's 2020 Budget:

DOT is responsible for supporting and enabling a high functioning transportation system—to move both people and goods safely and efficiently in order to support jobs and economic growth. The Budget supports necessary investments that ensure the Nation's air, surface, and maritime transportation systems are safe.

The Budget also funds initiatives to improve the condition and performance of the Nation's transportation infrastructure. In 2018 and 2019, DOT received large discretionary increases for surface transportation and airport infrastructure investments, meeting the Administration's call for increased infrastructure investments. The 2020 Budget continues certain important transportation infrastructure investments, but in a way that also recognizes that the Federal Government is not—and should not be—the primary funder of the Nation's transportation systems. The Budget also proposes robust competitive funding for programs that fund projects of national- or regional-significance, or that would result in improved safety outcomes. In addition, DOT will be bolstering its capabilities necessary to improve the efficiency and effectiveness of policy, economic analysis, and regulatory reform.

Invests in America's Surface Transportation Infrastructure. The 2020 Budget fully funds Highway Trust Fund-supported programs at levels consistent with the fifth and final year of the FAST Act. The Administration looks forward to working with the Congress to enact a long-term surface transportation reauthorization to follow the FAST Act. A long-term bill is necessary to

Invests in Emerging Transportation Technologies

DOT must keep pace with emerging entrants and technologies such as Unmanned Aircraft Systems (UAS), commercial space transportation, and autonomous vehicles, to ensure that the transformative benefits of these emerging technologies are realized. The Budget supports key investments in the Federal Aviation Administration (FAA) to expand the integration of UAS into the National Airspace and develop tools to automate the launch and reentry of commercial space operations and improve the efficiency of the launch license process. For autonomous vehicles, which could revolutionize the Nation's surface transportation system, DOT has had a number of important accomplishments, including the release of the Department's multimodal *Preparing for the Future of Transportation: Automated Vehicles 3.0* guidance document, which will help the private sector, States, and localities continue research and deployment activities safely. The Department will continue efforts in 2020 to enable the safe testing and integration of autonomous vehicles within the Nation's transportation systems by reducing regulatory barriers and conducting research.

provide certainty to America's State, local, and private partners, so they can plan and invest in projects with confidence. In addition, the 2020 Budget includes $200 billion for additional infrastructure investments. The Administration will work with the Congress on allocating this funding, to advance projects that provide the most benefit to Americans.

Prioritizes the Safety of the Nation's Transportation System. The Budget funds important investments to ensure the safety of the Nation's aviation, surface transportation, and maritime transportation networks. The Nation has made good progress in reducing overall transportation-related fatalities and injuries during the past two decades. Through its oversight of safety standards, outreach, and investments, DOT is committed to continuing this trend. The majority of transportation-related fatalities occur on the Nation's highways: 37,133 in 2017. To help address this issue, the Budget provides the Federal Highway Administration's Highway Safety Improvement Program with $2.7 billion. The Budget also provides FAST Act authorized funding of $929 million to the National Highway Traffic Safety Administration and $676 million to the Federal Motor Carrier Safety Administration to reduce fatalities and improve the safety of the Nation's infrastructure.

Emphasizes Competitive Programs that Generate Large Returns on Investment. The Budget makes targeted investments emphasizing innovation, leveraging, and partnerships to improve the Nation's surface transportation infrastructure. The Budget provides $1 billion to the Better Utilizing Investments to Leverage Development competitive grant program, which supports innovative projects that enhance quality of life and economic competitiveness in communities across the Nation, particularly in rural areas. The Budget allocates $2 billion to the Infrastructure for Rebuilding America (INFRA) competitive grant program, which is a $1 billion increase above the FAST Act-authorized level. The INFRA program has been successful in providing the seed money necessary to spur non-Federal investment in large projects that relieve congestion on the Nation's strategic multimodal freight network. The Budget includes $300 million in competitive highway bridge grants, which would reward States that use innovative and efficient procurement practices to repair or replace rural bridges that are in poor condition.

Modernizes FAA Infrastructure. The Budget invests $3.3 billion in FAA infrastructure. Modernizing the Nation's air traffic control infrastructure would improve the safety of the Nation's airspace, while reducing flight delays. Specifically, FAA would invest $136 million to further expand its Data Communication program, which would improve the communication between controllers and pilots across all phases of flight. The Budget would also invest $127 million to support the safe integration of unmanned aerial systems into the Nation's airspace, ensuring that the United States remains the world's aviation leader for decades to come.

Significantly Improves Amtrak and Rural Transportation Services. Amtrak's network has not been significantly modified since Amtrak's inception over 40 years ago, and long distance routes continually underperform, suffering from low ridership and large operating losses of roughly half a billion dollars annually. Simply put, Amtrak trains inadequately serve many rural markets while not serving many growing metropolitan areas at all. The Administration believes that restructuring the Amtrak system can result in better service (at a lower cost) by focusing trains on shorter distance (less than 750 miles) routes, while providing robust intercity bus service to currently underserved rural areas via a partnership between Amtrak and bus operators. To accomplish this transformation, the Budget provides $550 million in transitional grants as States and Amtrak begin the process to restructure the network and States prepare to incrementally take financial responsibility for the newly created State-supported routes. The Budget also provides $936 million in direct grants to Amtrak, to support investment on the Northeast Corridor and existing State-supported lines, and to assist Amtrak in this transition.

Leveraging Federal Investment for Critical Projects

The INFRA program, which makes awards to large projects that relieve congestion and reduce freight bottlenecks, is an example of how DOT effectively "leverages" Federal dollars to maximize overall investment in top priority infrastructure projects. For example, in 2018, DOT awarded a $184 million grant (paired with $70 million from other Federal sources) to an express lanes highway project in Georgia that has an estimated total cost of $1.6 billion. In the second round of INFRA awards, each Federal dollar invested in an INFRA project was matched by $1.65 in investment by State, local, and private partners.

Focuses the Capital Investment Grants (CIG) Program on the Most Impactful Projects. The CIG program supports the construction of new, or extensions of, fixed guideway transit, commuter rail, light rail, and bus rapid transit projects. The Administration believes that the program needs to be refocused on projects that have high non-Federal funding commitments and provide the greatest impact to improving mobility and access for riders who depend on public transit. The Budget includes $1.5 billion for the CIG program, which includes $500 million in funding for new projects.

Reforms the Essential Air Service (EAS) Program. EAS provides subsidized commercial air service to rural airports. Originally designed as a temporary program 40 years ago, today many EAS flights are left unfilled and obtain high per passenger subsidy costs. In addition, several EAS eligible communities are relatively close to major airports. The Budget proposes to reduce the discretionary funding for EAS and reform the program to target Federal funds for communities most in need of their services. The Budget would continue the mandatory resources for EAS at approximately $145 million.

Invests in Information Technology (IT) Transformation. The Budget builds on the work started in 2018 to consolidate and transform the Department's IT efforts to better support the Department's mission, strengthen cyber security, and achieve greater efficiencies in IT across DOT's Operating Administrations. The Budget proposes $502 million for DOT's Working Capital Fund, which would allow the Department to continue to consolidate IT investments into the Office of the Secretary of Transportation.

DEPARTMENT OF THE TREASURY

Funding Highlights:

- The Department of the Treasury (Treasury) manages the U.S. Government's finances, promotes conditions that enable stable economic growth, protects the integrity of the financial system, and combats financial crimes and terrorist financing.
- The Budget proposes reforms to bring greater accountability and efficiency to Treasury's operations and requests targeted new investments to protect the Nation from malign economic and cyber intrusions, secure and modernize the taxpayer experience, and lower the deficit.
- The Budget requests $12.7 billion in base discretionary resources for Treasury's domestic programs, a $0.2 billion or 1-percent decrease from the 2019 estimate.
- The Budget also proposes a program integrity initiative to narrow the gap between taxes owed and taxes paid that is estimated to reduce the deficit by $33 billion over 10 years.

The President's 2020 Budget:

The President's Budget would improve stewardship of taxpayer dollars by focusing on the Department's core economic and financial responsibilities. The Budget prioritizes resources to combat terrorist financing, proliferation financing, and other forms of illicit finance. The Budget also supports Treasury's role as chair of the Committee on Foreign Investment in the United States (CFIUS) to address current and future national security risks. In addition, the Budget invests in the Department's functions as the Federal Government's revenue collector, financial manager, and economic policymaker. The Budget would ensure that taxpayers, investors, and job-creators operate in an economy that is secure, fair, and free from unnecessary bureaucratic impediments.

Strengthens Review of Foreign Investments. CFIUS, a multi-agency body chaired by the Secretary of the Treasury, determines potential national security risks arising from certain foreign investments. The Foreign Investment Risk Review Modernization Act (FIRRMA), enacted in 2018, expands CFIUS's jurisdiction and strengthens its authorities to protect critical U.S. technologies and infrastructure from new and evolving threats, while preserving an open investment environment. The Budget requests $35 million for Treasury, as CFIUS chair, to ensure swift, robust, and effective implementation of FIRRMA.

Prioritizes Safeguarding Markets and Protecting Financial Data. Treasury's Office of Terrorism and Financial Intelligence (TFI) possesses a unique set of authorities and tools to combat terrorists, rogue regimes, proliferators of weapons of mass destruction, and other illicit actors by denying their access to the financial system, disrupting their revenue streams, and degrading their capabilities to inflict harm. The Financial Crimes Enforcement Network (FinCEN) links law enforcement and the intelligence communities with financial institutions and regulators facilitating the discovery and prosecution of illegal activities and money-laundering schemes.

The Budget requests $167 million for TFI to continue its work safeguarding the financial system from abuse and combatting other national security threats using economic sanctions. These funds would support TFI's growing workforce through critical investments in information technology and mission-support capabilities. The Budget requests $125 million for FinCEN to administer the Bank Secrecy Act and focus on the prevention of terrorist financing, money laundering, and other financial crimes. These resources would expand FinCEN's special measures enforcement activities and enhance its efforts to combat cybercrime and cryptocurrency threats.

The Budget also requests $18 million to protect Treasury information technology (IT) systems that carry out these activities, as well as those that account for and process trillions of dollars in revenue and payments against cybersecurity threats. These funds are requested in addition to bureau-level investments, and would be centrally managed to strengthen the security of Treasury's highest-value IT assets and improve Treasury's response and recovery capabilities.

The U.S. financial services sector faces a range of cybersecurity vulnerabilities and physical hazards. The Nation's adversaries have grown in technical capability, and their attacks have increased in sophistication. The Budget requests $13 million for the Office of Critical Infrastructure Protection and Compliance Policy to enhance the Department's capacity to identify and remediate new vulnerabilities before they can be exploited.

Invests in a 21st Century Internal Revenue Service (IRS). The IRS collects approximately $3.5 trillion in tax revenue annually and processes more than 253 million tax returns and forms resulting in more than $464 billion in tax refunds. The Budget proposes $11.5 billion in base funding for IRS to ensure that IRS can fulfill its core tax filing season responsibilities, continue critical IT modernization efforts, and provide acceptable levels of taxpayer service.

The Budget also proposes legislation enabling additional funding for new and continuing investments to expand and strengthen tax enforcement. These additional proposed investments are estimated to generate approximately $47 billion in additional revenue at a cost of $15 billion, yielding a net savings of $33 billion over 10 years. The Budget also includes several proposals to ensure that taxpayers comply with their obligations and that tax refunds are only paid to those who are eligible, including: improving oversight of paid tax preparers; giving IRS the authority to correct more errors on tax returns before refunds are issued; requiring a valid Social Security Number for work in order to claim certain tax credits; and increasing wage and information reporting.

The Budget provides $290 million for the IRS's multiyear IT modernization efforts, including upgrading its antiquated infrastructure and integrating its multiple case management and tax processing systems. Approximately 90 percent of individual taxpayers file their taxes electronically and can check on the status of their funds electronically. However, for most other taxpayer interactions, taxpayers and the IRS must interact through the mail, which slows the resolution of issues. These funds would also be used to increase taxpayers' ability to interact with IRS securely and electronically, improving the time it takes for IRS to resolve concerns.

Manages the Nation's Finances More Effectively. The Bureau of the Fiscal Service (Fiscal Service) conducts all Treasury debt financing operations, provides central payment services for Federal agencies, runs Government-wide accounting and reporting services, and manages the collection of delinquent debt. In 2018, the Fiscal Service issued approximately $10 trillion in marketable Treasury securities, processed the collection of more than $4 trillion in Federal receipts, and distributed more than $3.5 trillion in payments, including Social Security payments, IRS tax refunds, and veterans' benefits. The Budget supports increased efforts to monitor and protect the vital IT systems that implement these critical functions.

The Fiscal Service performs the vast majority of payment and collection transactions electronically, but in 2018, it still issued almost 56 million paper checks and collected more than $592 billion in payments by mail or in person. The Budget supports Treasury's efforts to move more payments to electronic methods to increase options for citizens and customers to conduct transactions with the Federal Government in a secure and more convenient electronic environment. It also includes proposals to help the Fiscal Service improve payment integrity.

Increases Treasury's Efficiency and Effectiveness by Streamlining Operations. The Budget eliminates funding for Community Development Financial Institutions (CDFI) Fund discretionary grant and direct loan programs. More than two decades ago, the CDFI Fund was created to jumpstart an industry at a time when CDFIs had limited access to private capital. The industry has now matured and has ready access to the capital needed to extend credit and provide financial services to underserved communities.

Brings Accountability and Transparency to Treasury's Regulatory Oversight Functions. The Budget proposes that the Congress establish funding levels for the Office of Financial Research (OFR) and the Financial Stability Oversight Council (FSOC) through annual appropriations bills. OFR and FSOC, established by the Dodd-Frank Act, are currently able to set their own budgets, which circumvents congressional approval and oversight. Bringing OFR and FSOC into the congressional appropriations process is consistent with recommendations made in Treasury's June 2017 report to the President on banks and credit unions. OFR has taken administrative steps to further the goals laid out in the Treasury report, including initiating an organizational realignment that has resulted in significant reductions to its staffing and operating expenses. In addition, Treasury is continuing efforts to make FSOC decision-making procedures more transparent and to implement more rigorous cost-benefit analysis standards.

The Federal Insurance Office within Treasury is coordinating with State insurance regulators and insurance industry groups to improve oversight and administration of the Terrorism Risk Insurance Program (TRIP), consistent with Treasury's October 2017 report to the President on asset management and insurance. Treasury is also evaluating reforms, to be included in any legislation extending TRIP beyond its current sunset date of December 31, 2020, to further decrease taxpayer exposure.

Streamlines Oversight of Alcohol and Tobacco Industries. The Budget proposes to transfer all alcohol and tobacco responsibilities from the Department of Justice's Bureau of Alcohol, Tobacco, Firearms and Explosives (ATF) to Treasury's Alcohol and Tobacco Tax and Trade Bureau (TTB). This transfer would leverage TTB's resources and expertise relating to the alcohol and tobacco industries and allow ATF to continue to focus on its firearms and explosives mandates, enabling both agencies to more efficiently and effectively carry out their core mission of protecting the public.

Consolidates and Streamlines Federal Financial Literacy and Education Efforts. The Budget proposes that Federal efforts to promote financial literacy focus on the high-impact areas of: basic financial capability; housing; higher education; military and veteran programs; and investment and retirement planning. More than 20 Federal agencies have some form of financial education or literacy programs. Collectively, Federal agencies spent an estimated $250 million on financial literacy and education activities in 2017. Streamlining and consolidating programs and activities would be a multiyear effort.

DEPARTMENT OF VETERANS AFFAIRS

Funding Highlights:

- The Department of Veterans Affairs (VA) is committed to providing military veterans and their survivors with the benefits, care, and support they have earned through sacrifice and service to the Nation.
- The 2020 Budget fulfills the President's promise by making critical investments in high priority initiatives that ensure veterans receive top quality care, benefits, and services—wherever they work or live. The Budget provides dedicated resources to implement the historic VA MISSION Act of 2018 and gives veterans greater choice and access to the medical care they deserve. The Budget also provides resources to improve the veteran experience across all programs and services, as well as promote efficiency, transparency, and accountability within the Department.
- The Budget requests $93.1 billion for VA, a $6.5 billion or 7.5-percent increase from the 2019 enacted level. In addition, the Budget requests $87.6 billion in advance appropriations for VA medical care programs in 2021 to ensure the Department has sufficient resources to continue providing the premier services that veterans have earned. The request also includes new legislative authorities and $123.1 billion in mandatory budget authority, including $129.5 billion in 2021 advance appropriations for other critical veteran and survivor benefits.

The President's 2020 Budget:

VA's mission is to deliver world-class benefits, care, and support to America's military veterans, their families, and survivors. The Budget provides the necessary resources to meet the Nation's commitment to veterans to help them recover from illnesses, injuries, or wounds sustained in service and to enable their successful reintegration into civilian life.

The Budget fully funds VA to operate one of the largest integrated healthcare systems in the United States with over 9.3 million enrolled veterans, provide disability compensation benefits to nearly 5.5 million veterans and their survivors, and administer pension benefits for approximately 440,000 veterans and their survivors.

In addition, the Budget makes investments across a broad range of veteran services and programs including: educational assistance for nearly one million students; rehabilitation and employment benefits for approximately 149,000 veterans; servicemember and veteran group life insurance plans for approximately six million enrollees; home mortgages, including more than three million active loans; and memorial and burial benefits in more than 137 national cemeteries and thousands of other cemeteries across the Nation.

Expands Veterans' Choice and Access to Medical Care

Invests in World-Class Healthcare. The Budget proposes $80.2 billion to fully fund VA medical care requirements in 2020, a $7.0 billion or 9.6-percent increase from the 2019 enacted level. The Budget also proposes $87.6 billion in advance appropriations for VA medical care programs in 2021.

> *"Our Nation's veterans fulfilled their duty to this country with brave and loyal service; it is our moral and solemn obligation to demonstrate to them our continuing gratitude, unwavering support, and meaningful encouragement."*
>
> President Donald J. Trump
> October 31, 2018

Implements the VA MISSION Act of 2018. The Budget fully supports implementation of the VA MISSION Act of 2018 and provides veterans greater choice on where they receive their healthcare—whether at VA or through a private healthcare provider. The Budget consolidates all veterans' community care programs into a single program, reducing bureaucracy and making it easier for veterans to navigate their healthcare needs.

Increases Veterans' Access to Urgent Care and Expands the Caregivers Program. As part of the VA MISSION Act of 2018, the Budget supports VA's brand new urgent care benefit. Veterans would be able to use more convenient, urgent care facilities in the community, often times closer to home. The Budget also supports the VA MISSION Act of 2018's expansion of the Caregivers program to include eligible veterans who incurred or aggravated a serious injury in the line of duty before September 11, 2001. Expansion of the Caregivers program would coincide with new information technology (IT) updates necessary to effectively manage the program.

Prioritizes Funding for Suicide Prevention. Reducing deaths by suicide among the Nation's veterans continues to be VA's top clinical priority. The Budget provides essential resources for VA's suicide prevention programs and supports the expansion of key initiatives aimed at advancing VA's National Strategy for Preventing Veteran Suicide.

Improves the Veteran Experience

Provides Critical Funding for IT. The Budget provides $4.3 billion for essential investments in IT to improve the online interface between the veteran and the Department. This includes an increase of more than $200 million to recapitalize aging network infrastructure, to expedite VA's transition to the cloud, and to support emerging VA MISSION Act of 2018 IT requirements.

In addition, the Budget includes $1.6 billion as part of a multiyear effort to continue implementation of a new Electronic Health Record (EHR) system. The EHR is a high-priority initiative that would ensure a seamlessly integrated healthcare record between the Department of Defense and VA, by bringing all patient data into one common system.

> *"More importantly, the interoperability of the new electronic health records system will connect VA to the DOD, private doctors and private pharmacies to create a continuum of care and organize the healthcare around our veteran's needs."*
>
> Robert L. Wilkie
> Secretary
> June 27, 2018

Addresses Infrastructure Deficiencies. The Budget provides $1.6 billion for VA's construction program to complete high priority major and minor construction projects. More than $1.2 billion is provided to begin construction of a new hospital in Louisville, KY, complete construction of other ongoing major medical facilities, make critical seismic corrections, and expand

VA's national cemeteries. An additional $399 million would be used to renovate existing office and patient care space across the Department. The Budget also provides $1.2 billion for non-recurring maintenance projects to maintain and modernize medical facilities. These critical investments enhance the safety and security of VA facilities, help implement new patient-centered designs, and ensure VA programs and services keep pace with modern technologies.

Modernizes the Veteran Appeals Process. The Budget provides sufficient resources for the Board of Veterans Appeals and the Veterans Benefits Administration to implement the Veterans Appeals Improvement and Modernization Act of 2017, a new streamlined framework that will provide quicker decisions on new veteran compensation appeals and resolve the remaining legacy appeals inventory. The new framework will provide veterans with increased options to resolve their appeals and improve the timeliness of appeals decisions.

Increases Access to Burial and Memorial Benefits. The Budget includes $329 million, a 4.2-percent increase from the 2019 enacted level, to expand veteran access to memorial benefits, deliver premier services to veterans' families, and provide perpetual care for more than 3.9 million gravesites. This funding would sustain 144 cemeteries and sites, including the initial activation of five new cemeteries to support VA's goal of providing veterans with a burial option within 75 miles of their home. The Budget also funds the transfer of 11 cemeteries from the Department of Defense as part of the President's *Delivering Government Solutions in the 21st Century* plan. In addition, the Budget increases funding by $13 million to improve customer service, responsiveness, and efforts to better memorialize veterans and tell their stories.

Promotes Efficiency, Transparency, and Accountability

Targets Investments to Create Efficiencies. The Budget prioritizes investments in areas that would create cost savings over time, as well as improve the efficiency and effectiveness of VA programs. Targeted investments to IT systems, to include more than $200 million for cloud migration and replacing aging infrastructure to support the new EHR system, would result in cost savings as VA consolidates data centers and reallocates resources to higher priority needs. VA is also committed to modernizing the disability compensation program and identifying innovative pilot programs aimed at providing meaningful empowerment opportunities for disabled veterans seeking employment.

Streamlines Government. The Budget promotes fiscal discipline by implementing Federal reorganization proposals that would more effectively and efficiently utilize taxpayer funds. The Budget better aligns small business certification programs across Government by ensuring proper management of Service Disabled Veteran Owned Small Business certification programs under the Small Business Administration.

Reduces Waste, Fraud, and Abuse. The Budget provides $229 million for VA programs designed to improve oversight, accountability, and performance within the Department. This includes $22 million, a 25-percent increase from the 2019 enacted level, in direct funding for the Office of Accountability and Whistleblower Protection. Since the President's signing of the Department of Veterans Affairs Accountability and Whistleblower Protection Act of 2017, which has allowed the Department to more efficiently discipline poor-performing VA employees, more than 4,300 employees have been removed, demoted, or suspended. The Budget also provides $207 million, a 7.8-percent increase above the 2019 enacted level, for the Office of the Inspector General to strengthen accountability, promote transparency, and reduce waste, fraud, and abuse.

CORPS OF ENGINEERS—CIVIL WORKS

Funding Highlights:

- The Army Corps of Engineers civil works program (Corps) develops, manages, restores, and protects water resources primarily through the construction, operation and maintenance, and study of water-related infrastructure projects. The Corps is also responsible for regulating development on navigable waters of the United States and works with other Federal agencies to help communities respond to and recover from floods and other natural disasters.
- The Budget focuses Federal investment where it is most warranted within the three primary mission areas of the Corps to address the most significant risks to public safety or to provide a high economic or environmental return to the Nation. The Budget also proposes reforms to how the Nation invests in water resources projects, reducing the reliance on Federal funding and control and providing State and local governments, as well as the private sector, more flexibility to make investments they deem a priority.
- The Budget requests $4.8 billion for the Corps, a $2.2 billion or 31-percent decrease from the 2019 enacted level.

The President's 2020 Budget:

The Corps has three main missions: flood and storm damage reduction; commercial navigation; and aquatic ecosystem restoration. The Corps also regulates development in navigable waters and wetlands. While the Agency has had a significant impact on water resources development throughout its history, current approaches to funding, constructing, and maintaining projects often do not deliver benefits in either a timely or cost-effective manner. The current paradigm for investing in water resources development is not optimal; it can deter rather than enable local communities, States, and the private sector from making important investments on their own, even when they are the primary beneficiaries. The Budget lays the foundation for accelerating the construction of infrastructure and increasing competition in the delivery of projects, thereby resulting in faster completion of projects and cost savings. The Budget focuses Federal resources where they are most warranted, encourages more non-Federal leadership, and removes barriers that can impede the ability of non-Federal parties to move forward on their own with investments in water resources infrastructure they deem priorities.

Invests in America's Future

Emphasizes Investments in Ongoing Construction of Projects that Address a Significant Risk to Public Safety or Provide a High Economic or Environmental Return. The Budget keeps the Federal Government's promise to complete ongoing construction projects that provide a high return to the Nation or address a significant risk to public safety more quickly and at a more effective cost. By proposing not to start any new construction projects, the Budget enables the Corps to focus on completing these ongoing priority projects faster and at a reduced cost, allowing the affected communities to see their benefits sooner. The Budget also recognizes the need to change the way future construction investments are funded with less reliance on Federal appropriations. For example, the Budget provides $150 million for innovative partnerships between the Federal Government and non-Federal sponsors to accelerate completion of projects.

Prioritizes Operating and Maintaining Existing Infrastructure. The Budget gives priority to operating and maintaining existing water resources infrastructure and improving its reliability. Maintenance of the key features of this infrastructure is funded; this includes navigation channels that serve the Nation's largest coastal ports and the inland waterways with the most commercial use, such as the Mississippi and Ohio Rivers and the Illinois Waterway.

Transforming How Water Resources Infrastructure is Delivered for the Nation

"For the first time, the work plan provides funds for two projects where the local sponsor could use [s]ection 1043 of the Water Resources Reform and Development Act of 2014 to complete project construction. This section authorizes [Corps] to provide its share of a project's construction costs directly to a non-[F]ederal sponsor who is able to assume responsibility for construction of a [Corps] project."—*Army Corps of Engineers FY 2018 Work Plan* press release, June 11, 2018. The Budget builds on this progress, providing $150 million in funding for non-Federal sponsors that propose to construct projects on their own under section 1043 of the Water Resources Reform and Development Act of 2014, as amended.

Promotes More Local Control in Constructing Water Resources Projects. The Budget expands the Corps's current use of section 1043 of the Water Resources Reform and Development Act of 2014, as amended, by including $150 million for an innovative program under which the Corps would transfer appropriated funds to non-Federal sponsors that decide to construct a project on their own. Non-Federal implementation of projects, where appropriate, would accelerate the construction of more infrastructure projects and create efficiencies in their delivery. Under this program, the Corps would issue a solicitation for proposals from non-Federal sponsors to construct their own projects using a combination of Federal and non-Federal funding. Other projects specifically funded in the Budget may also qualify for implementation under section 1043. The Budget also proposes to extend section 1043 which, under current law, expires in 2019.

Respects and Protects American Taxpayers

Reforms Inland Waterways Funding. The Budget proposes to reform the laws governing the Inland Waterways Trust Fund, including an annual per-vessel fee for commercial users, to help finance future capital investments on these waterways and a portion of the cost of operating and maintaining them. The current diesel fuel tax is insufficient to support the users' share of these costs.

Divests the Washington Aqueduct. The Budget proposes to sell the Washington Aqueduct, the wholesale supply system for Washington D.C.; Arlington County, Virginia; the City of Falls Church, Virginia; and parts of Fairfax County, Virginia. The Corps owns and operates the Aqueduct, which is the only local water supply system in the Nation owned and operated by the Corps. Ownership of local water supply is best carried out by a State or local government, or by the private sector where there are appropriate market and regulatory incentives. Selling the Aqueduct to a public or private utility would contribute to American prosperity through a more efficient allocation of economic resources.

Increases Accountability. The Budget establishes clear priorities based on objective criteria for investment decisions. This approach ensures the best overall use of available funds and allows the American taxpayer to understand how Federal resources are allocated. For example, the Budget funds dam safety studies and dredged material management plans within the Investigations account, instead of the Operation and Maintenance account, where they appropriately belong. The Budget also classifies the Poplar Island project, which serves as the primary dredged-material disposal site for the Port of Baltimore, as a navigation project.

Working with States and Local Communities to Improve Infrastructure

The Budget funds transfer of ownership of the Kentucky River Locks and Dams 1, 2, 3, and 4, to the Kentucky River Association. Transferring infrastructure such as these locks and dams, which no longer serve a Federal role, to the primary beneficiaries enables greater local control and management of infrastructure that is important to the local communities.

Increases Fiscal Discipline and Transparency. The Budget proposes revisions to the appropriations language for the Construction, Operation and Maintenance, and Mississippi River and Tributaries accounts, and new appropriations language for the Harbor Maintenance and Inland Waterways Trust Funds, to provide greater transparency in how these funds are spent. Establishing separate appropriations accounts for the navigation trust funds would improve accountability, ensure appropriations are used for the purpose for which the Congress intended, and increase transparency for the public, including the users that pay fees to finance some of these costs.

ENVIRONMENTAL PROTECTION AGENCY

Funding Highlights:

- The Environmental Protection Agency (EPA) is responsible for implementing and enforcing statutes designed to protect human health and the environment.
- The 2020 Budget continues EPA's work to ensure clean air, water, and land, and safer chemicals, while reducing regulatory burden and eliminating lower-priority activities. Focusing on the core mission makes EPA a better steward of taxpayer dollars and promotes operational efficiencies that enhance the Agency's performance.
- The Budget requests \$6.1 billion for EPA, a \$2.8 billion or 31-percent decrease from the 2019 estimate.

The President's 2020 Budget:

Environmental protection and public health are key to U.S. prosperity and essential to America's quality of life. Through cooperative federalism, EPA works with States and Tribes, as well as local governments, businesses, and the public to protect human health and the environment.

The Budget proposes to eliminate many voluntary and lower-priority activities and refocus the Agency on strategic and regulatory reforms such as implementation of:

- Cooperative federalism activities under various environmental statutes;
- Requirements under Executive Order 13807, "One Federal Decision;"
- Activities to support attainment of the national ambient air quality standards and implementation of air toxics standards;
- Waters of the United States (WOTUS) definitional changes;
- The 2016 Amendments to the Toxic Substances Control Act (TSCA); and
- The Affordable Clean Energy rule, a replacement to the Obama-era Clean Power Plan.

Continues Focus on Core Agency Activities. The Budget maintains EPA's focus on its core mission—providing Americans with clean air, land, and water, and ensuring chemical safety. EPA will continue streamlining programs and processes, eliminating many voluntary and lower-priority activities, and empowering States and Tribes as the primary implementers of environmental programs. This prioritization supports an efficient, effective approach that will provide tangible environmental results for the American people within the scope of EPA's core statutory obligations.

Promotes Regulatory and Permitting Reforms, and Enhances Cooperative Federalism. The Budget provides resources to ensure EPA is able to meet pressing demands in priority areas including reviewing and revising regulations, improving the permitting process, and enhancing collaboration with State, tribal, and Federal partners. For example, several significant rulemakings are expected to be completed before 2020, including replacement rules for WOTUS and the 2015 Clean Power Plan. EPA will work to provide technical assistance and implementation guidance to States, Tribes, and regulated entities as they adapt to these changes. Efforts to identify and address potential hold-ups in the permitting process will also continue, to ensure that unnecessary delays do not get in the way of environmental protection or economic growth. In addition, EPA will promote joint governance in order to enhance shared accountability between EPA, States, and Tribes, including facilitating and promoting the delegation of environmental programs.

Supports Healthier Schools. Approximately 50 million American children spend their time in K-12 school facilities every day. Many of these buildings are old and contain environmental hazards that could pose a risk to children's health. To address this issue, the Budget establishes a $50 million multi-media grant program to identify and help resolve these hazards. Activities supported by this grant program would result in safer and healthier school environments for American children.

User Fee Proposals

By administering select EPA programs through the collection of user fees, entities benefiting from those programs would directly pay for the services and benefits that the programs provide. The 2020 Budget outlines legislative proposals to authorize EPA to administer a handful of mature programs through the collection and expenditure of user fees. For instance, the Budget includes a proposal to fee-fund the ENERGY STAR program, a voluntary certification program that aims to help businesses and individuals save money and protect the environment through improved energy efficiency. Other proposals would authorize EPA to collect and spend fees to provide compliance assistance services related to risk management and spill prevention and response planning at industrial facilities. The Budget also includes a proposal to expand the range of activities that EPA can fund with existing pesticide registration service fees and maintenance fees.

Sets and Implements Appropriate Air Pollution Standards. The Budget funds EPA's activities to control air pollution and radiation exposure at $425 million. Prioritizing funding would help reduce the number of areas of nonattainment across the Nation, ensuring that the United States continues to lead the world in having both clean air and a strong economy. EPA will continue its implementation of national air quality standards and, in close collaboration with States and Tribes, will seek to improve the efficiency and effectiveness of State Implementation Plan review processes. In addition, funding for EPA's vehicle programs would support the review of approximately 5,000 vehicle and engine emissions certification requests.

Strengthens Protections from Toxic Chemicals. In 2016, the Congress passed the Frank R. Lautenberg Chemical Safety for the 21st Century Act to modernize TSCA. TSCA, as amended, requires EPA to evaluate whether existing chemicals may pose unreasonable risks and, if so, take immediate steps to protect human health and the environment. EPA must also affirm that new chemicals entering the market are safe and that appropriate measures are taken to address risks. In 2020, this work would accelerate as the Agency reaches statutory deadlines to complete the first set of risk evaluations for existing chemicals and begins the next phase of work. The Budget provides support to these efforts, which would supplement fees paid by chemical manufacturers and processors.

Invests in Water Infrastructure Construction, Repair, and Replacement. The Budget funds water infrastructure through the State Revolving Funds, the Water Infrastructure Finance and Innovation Act (WIFIA) credit program, and the recently authorized America's Water Infrastructure Act (AWIA). The 2020 capitalization of the State Revolving Funds would supplement approximately $80 billion currently revolving at the State level. Credit subsidy funding for WIFIA would continue the program's momentum by supporting more than $2 billion in direct loans which, when combined with other funding sources, would spur more than $4 billion in total water infrastructure investment. In addition, the Budget proposes funds for AWIA grant programs that would assist in lead testing and drinking water fountain replacement in schools, sewer overflow control, and water infrastructure workforce investment. These resources would complement State and local drinking water and wastewater infrastructure investments as well as funding provided through other Federal channels.

Optimizes the Approach to Clean-Up Efforts at the Nation's Most Complex Hazardous Waste Sites. The Budget provides $1 billion for the Hazardous Substance Superfund Account to address the release of hazardous substances and clean up hazardous waste sites. With EPA on track to complete all of the recommendations made in EPA's Superfund Task Force Report by the end of 2019, the Budget supports the full implementation of the optimized approach to cleaning up Superfund sites. EPA has made significant progress identifying impediments to expeditious clean up at sites with significant exposure risks and developing action plans to overcome those impediments. EPA is also working with prospective purchasers, developers, and responsible parties to bring more private funding for redevelopment, saving taxpayer dollars for the sites that truly need Federal funding. Reducing exposure to hazardous substances and revitalizing contaminated land for use by the community is a priority for the Administration and a fundamental part of EPA's core mission.

Making Decisions and Saving Taxpayer Dollars

In meeting its commitment to the community of Bridgeton, Missouri, EPA signed a final Record of Decision (ROD) setting forth a $205 million clean-up plan for the West Lake Landfill Superfund site. The ROD amends a controversial version from 2008 that caused a near stalemate in remedial activity at the site. EPA leadership identified this site as a priority and worked through the challenges to settle on a final remedy that will take less time to complete and cost $30 million less, while still maintaining the desired public health protections.

Reinforces Emergency Preparedness and Response Capabilities. Recognizing weather impacts on U.S. communities and intentional threats made against the homeland, the Administration continues to support capabilities across the Federal Government to prepare for and respond to these hazards. EPA plays a critical role in this capacity, providing technical assistance to drinking water and wastewater utilities, responding to the release of hazardous substances, and advising on disease vector control and waste disposal. Within the Hazardous Substance Superfund Account, the Budget supports EPA's efforts by providing $176 million to the Superfund Emergency Preparedness and Emergency Response and Removal programs, as well as $81 million for EPA's Homeland Security programs. This funding supports the development of hazard mitigation and resilience guidance, specialized regional emergency response planning documents, sampling methods, and decontamination technical support tools. Protecting the safety and security of the American people is a Federal priority that ensures a prosperous Nation.

Enhances Monitoring of America's Significant Watersheds. The Budget funds programs to measure and assess the health of the Great Lakes and Chesapeake Bay. These watersheds require coordination and collaboration among numerous States, Tribes, and local governments. In the case of the Great Lakes, international coordination is also necessary. The availability of accurate and continuous water quality data underpins ecosystem restoration efforts. The Budget provides support for basin-wide monitoring in these watersheds, including efforts to track and address harmful algal blooms and invasive species. These programs support cooperative federalism by building State and local capacity to conduct monitoring.

Supports Leading-Edge Research and Development for American Safety, Prosperity, and a Better Future. The Budget funds EPA's research and development activities in support of core mission areas, focusing on air quality, water resources, sustainable communities, chemical safety, and human health risk assessment. These interdisciplinary research programs provide the scientific foundation for EPA to execute its mandate to protect human health and the environment. EPA research programs also support cooperative federalism by developing new approaches and methodologies that States and Tribes leverage to address current and future environmental hazards. The Agency will continue aligning research resources to fulfill its statutory obligations and support EPA programs, regions, States, and Tribes in addressing their most pressing environmental and related public health challenges.

NATIONAL AERONAUTICS AND SPACE ADMINISTRATION

Funding Highlights:

- The National Aeronautics and Space Administration (NASA) is responsible for leading an innovative and sustainable program of exploration with commercial and international partners to enable human expansion across the solar system and bring new knowledge and opportunities back to Earth.
- The Budget takes steps to achieve lunar exploration goals sooner, improve sustainability of NASA's exploration campaign, and increase the use of commercial partnerships and other procurement models to enhance the efficiency and effectiveness of NASA programs.
- The Budget includes $363 million to support commercial development of a large lunar lander that can initially carry cargo and later astronauts to the surface of the Moon.
- The Budget focuses funding for the Space Launch System (SLS) rocket, a heavy-lift expendable launch vehicle, to ensure the rocket is operational in the early 2020s when it will be needed to carry astronauts to the vicinity of the Moon.
- The Budget requests $21 billion for NASA, a $283 million or 1.4-percent increase from the 2019 estimate.

The President's 2020 Budget:

NASA supports growth of the Nation's economy in space, increases understanding of the universe and America's place in it, works with industry to improve America's aerospace technologies, and advances American leadership. The Budget supports an innovative and sustainable program of space exploration by using novel approaches to partner closely with American industry, funding transformative technologies that will lower the cost and increase the capabilities of the Nation's space activities, while focusing on key capabilities to meet long-term exploration outcomes.

Continues Building the Key Components that Would Send Astronauts to the Moon and Beyond. The Budget proposes funding for key components of NASA's exploration campaign, including: the SLS and Orion crew capsule to support a first uncrewed test launch in the early 2020s and a steady crewed launch cadence thereafter; the Lunar Gateway, a small way station around the Moon in the mid-2020s; commercial launch capabilities to enable regular, low-cost access to the lunar vicinity and surface; and lunar landers to enable cargo delivery and human access to the lunar surface. The Budget proposes reforms to the SLS program to prevent the program's significant cost and schedule challenges from further diverting resources from other exploration activities. Most

> *"My Administration is reclaiming America's heritage as the world's greatest space-faring [N]ation. The essence of the American character is to explore new horizons and to tame new frontiers."*
>
> President Donald J. Trump
> June 18, 2018

notably, the Budget defers funding of upgrades (known as "Block 1B") for the SLS, and instead focuses the program on the completion of the initial version of the SLS and supporting a reliable SLS and Orion annual flight cadence. Lunar Gateway elements would be launched on competitively procured vehicles, complementing crew transport flights on the SLS and Orion. This approach would accelerate commercial lunar delivery capabilities critical to U.S. exploration objectives and speed up the timeline for lunar surface exploration.

Increases Funding for New Technologies, Partnerships, and Approaches to Accelerate Exploration while Making It More Affordable. The Budget supports robust funding for exploration technology research and development, with an increase in funding to support lunar surface activities. These efforts prioritize developing the capacity to understand and potentially utilize lunar resources to reduce transportation costs both to and from the Moon as well as to enhance lunar exploration capabilities. The Budget also supports use of commercial capabilities to deliver science and technology payloads to the Moon in preparation for future exploration. In addition, the Budget supports a major new initiative to support competitive commercial development of a large lander that would first carry cargo, and then crew, to the lunar surface.

Drives toward a Vibrant, U.S.-Led Economy in Earth Orbit. The Budget provides funding for the International Space Station as well as for new commercial space capabilities that will facilitate a transition to a more robust and cost-effective approach to human space activities near the Earth. By 2025, the Budget envisions commercial capabilities on the International Space Station as well as new commercial facilities and platforms to continue the American presence in Earth orbit. The Budget also increases funding for innovative activities conducted in orbit, including microgravity research and in-space robotic manufacturing and assembly. NASA would also expand its reliance on existing commercial space activity by creating a new Communications Services Program that would begin to purchase commercial communications services to return data generated by science missions back to Earth.

> *"President Trump and our entire Administration believe that America's prosperity, security, and even our national character, depend on American leadership in space. And over the past year, the world has seen the vital role that private enterprise plays to advance American leadership in outer space."*
>
> Michael R. Pence
> Vice President
> February 21, 2018

Supports an Ambitious Program of Solar System Exploration. The Budget provides $2.6 billion for Planetary Science, including approximately $600 million for a mission to Jupiter's moon Europa that would launch in 2023. By launching that mission on a commercial launch vehicle, NASA would save over $700 million, allowing multiple new activities to be funded across the Agency. The Budget would also initiate a mission to return samples from Mars, a top priority of the science community that also supports future human exploration. The Budget fully funds the James Webb Space Telescope, which is planned to be NASA's premier observatory of the next decade.

Replenishes Resources for Crosscutting Mission Support Activities. Each NASA mission rests on a sound foundation of institutional capabilities that keep the Agency functioning. The Budget increases investments in mission support areas such as facility maintenance, information technology and mission safety to ensure that critical services and assets are ready and reliable when needed. The Budget also funds numerous construction programs, including $126 million to consolidate research and production facilities at two NASA Centers.

Supports Transformative Aeronautics Technology Research. The Budget funds cutting-edge aeronautics research to boost U.S. technological and economic leadership and support high-quality American jobs. The Budget funds continued development of the X-59 Quiet Supersonic Technology demonstrator to usher in a new era of U.S.-led supersonic transportation. The Budget also supports development of capabilities that could be used to make commercial air travel more efficient, enables expanded operation of commercial unmanned vehicles in U.S. airspace, and begins a new partnership with industry to enable a potential new urban air mobility market.

Redirects Funds from Lower Priority Science and Education Programs to Higher Priorities. Consistent with prior budgets, the Budget provides no funding for the WFIRST space telescope, two Earth science missions, and the Office of Science, Technology, Engineering, and Mathematics (STEM) Engagement. Lower-cost STEM-related activities such as internships and robotics competitions funded outside of the Office of STEM Engagement continue to be supported.

SMALL BUSINESS ADMINISTRATION

Funding Highlights:

- The Small Business Administration (SBA) serves American entrepreneurs in their pursuit to start, grow, recover, and expand their businesses. As the Nation's leading advocate for small businesses, SBA ensures that business owners have access to affordable capital, mentoring and counseling opportunities, and immediate support in the wake of disaster.
- The Budget recognizes the vital role small businesses fulfill in contributing to the Nation's economic strength, building America's future, and helping the United States compete in today's marketplace. The Budget emphasizes the importance of investing in growing and recovering American communities while upholding SBA's commitment that its services are efficient, effective, and accountable.
- The Budget requests $820 million in new budget authority for 2020, a $119 million or 17-percent increase from the 2019 estimate. This request is offset by fiscally responsible proposals to provide SBA the flexibility to adjust existing fee structures across its business loan guarantee programs, resulting in a net request of $665 million, a $36 million or 5-percent decrease from the 2019 estimate.

The President's 2020 Budget:

Small businesses are the engines of the American economy. They are the job creators and innovators that fuel American neighborhoods and preserve U.S. prosperity. The SBA was established in 1953 to aid, counsel, assist, and protect the interests of small business concerns; preserve free competitive enterprise; and maintain and strengthen the overall economy of the Nation. Today, SBA continues to support the Nation's 30 million small businesses through an array of tailored programs and services. SBA's lending programs complement credit markets by meeting demand when economic shocks reduce commercial lending to small businesses, and when the private market is unwilling to offer capital to credit-worthy borrowers. Its nationwide network of private-sector and non-profit partners educate, advise, and inspire a new generation of entrepreneurs. In 2020, SBA will be uniquely positioned to leverage the Administration's pro-growth policies to equip small business owners with the right resources to be competitive in today's market and promote economic security for their businesses and families. The agency will fulfill this mission while promoting fiscal discipline by proposing policies that level the playing field with private sector support for small businesses.

Expands Opportunity for Small Business Owners. The Budget supports $43 billion in business lending to assist U.S. small business owners in accessing affordable capital to start, build, and grow their businesses. These products serve a variety of business needs, from funding general business operations like working capital and capital expenses, to fixed-asset financing for machinery and equipment, construction, and commercial real estate. They also provide the opportunity for small businesses to refinance existing loans. To ensure that SBA can provide these services without taxpayers subsidizing their costs, the Budget proposes that SBA have the flexibility to adjust fees across its business loan programs. This would allow the agency to finance both its anticipated lending and operational costs while ensuring it does not supplant services better provided solely by the private sector in periods of economic growth.

Strengthens Support to Entrepreneurs in Emerging Markets. The Budget would support greater outreach and lending to socially and economically disadvantaged urban communities and rural areas. In 2020, the SBA would build on its ongoing rural outreach efforts by adapting and developing new platforms to reach entrepreneurs in emerging markets. SBA would also work with other Federal agencies, such as the U.S. Departments of Agriculture and the Interior to improve program effectiveness and increase access to capital through enhanced collaboration and coordination.

> *"For many years, Washington tried to hold you back and tear you down, crushing the American small business with crippling taxes and oppressive regulation. But all that has changed starting in November 2016. The Trump [A]dministration is with you, and we are with you 100 percent. And always will be."*
>
> President Donald J. Trump
> June 19, 2018

Promotes Investment in the Nation's Newest Enterprises. Through its 7(m) Direct Microloan program, the SBA supports low-interest financing for non-profit intermediaries that in turn provide loans of up to $50,000 to the smallest of small businesses and start-ups. In addition to the $25 million in technical assistance grant funds requested for the Microloan program, the Budget requests $4 million in subsidy resources to support $40 million in direct lending.

Modernizes the Government's Role in Venture Capital. Created in 1958, the Small Business Investment Company (SBIC) program guarantees funds for privately owned and operated venture capital firms to make investments in small businesses. While the Budget supports $4 billion in new lending to continue this program, it also recognizes that the SBIC program has not kept pace with the evolution of the venture capital market, presenting an opportunity for sensible program reform. The Budget supports SBA's efforts to comprehensively evaluate the program to ensure SBICs provide innovative and modern financial products to American small businesses, regardless of their geographic location or industry focus.

Supports Recovery Efforts in the Wake of Disaster. SBA continues to be a vital resource for American households and businesses that need to recover quickly in the wake of disaster. In 2018, SBA approved more than 140,000 disaster loans totaling nearly $7 billion in financial support to American communities. The Budget continues to support more than $1 billion in direct, low-interest lending to business owners, homeowners, renters, and property owners.

Fosters Entrepreneurial Development and Education. SBA leverages its nationwide field personnel and diverse network of private sector and non-profit partners across each U.S. State and Territory to provide counseling, mentoring, and training assistance to nearly one million small business owners each year. The Budget requests $101 million for the Small Business Development Center program and proposes the creation of a competitive set-aside within this total to reward partners who most efficiently serve small businesses. The Budget continues to invest in counseling and mentoring programs such as Women's Business Centers, Veterans Outreach, and SCORE that provide essential coaching opportunities to developing small businesses and entrepreneurs.

Creates Fair Competition in Federal Contracting and Research. The ability to enter into contracts with the Federal Government is one of the most direct forms of financial support the Federal Government grants to U.S. small businesses. The Budget increases investment in SBA's 8(a) program to establish a full certification program for SBA's women-owned business certification programs. SBA continues to lead Federal efforts to deliver 23 percent of contracts to U.S. small businesses, which includes set-asides of five percent for women-owned and small, disadvantaged 8(a) businesses, and three percent for historically underutilized business zones and service-disabled veteran-owned businesses. The Budget also continues to support small business research and innovation by supporting competitive funding agreements through its Small Business Innovation Research program.

> *"The tax cuts spearheaded by President Trump mean more workers have gotten new jobs, raises, and bonuses – giving them more money to spend. Plus, as small businesses succeed, they create more revenue and more jobs for their communities – benefits that propel our economy and our [N]ation toward even greater prosperity."*
>
> Linda McMahon
> Administrator
> November 23, 2018

Advocates for the American Entrepreneur. The Budget supports $9.1 million for SBA's Office of Advocacy. As the independent voice for small business interests within the Federal Government, the Office of Advocacy promotes policies that minimize economic burdens faced by small business owners and analyzes the effects of proposed regulations and deregulatory efforts.

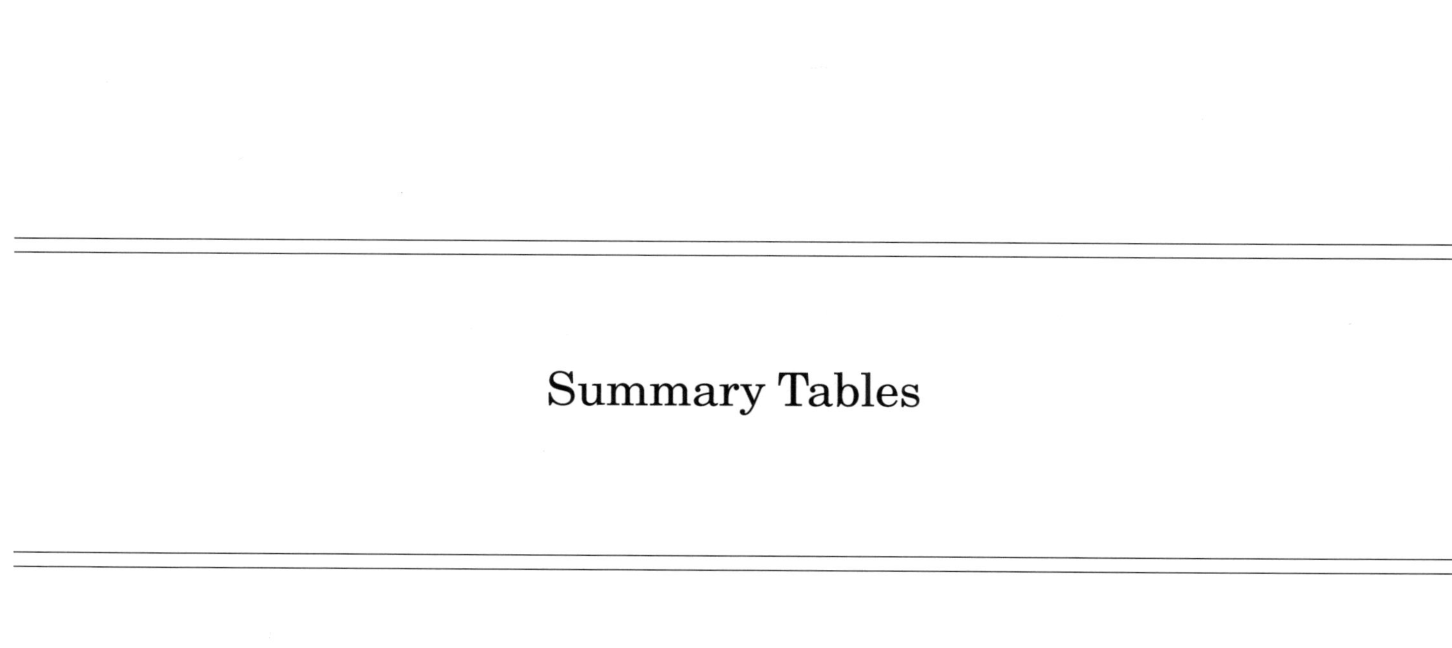

Summary Tables

Table S–1. Budget Totals

(In billions of dollars and as a percent of GDP)

	2018	2019	2020	2021	2022	2023	2024	2025	2026	2027	2028	2029	Totals 2020–2024	Totals 2020–2029
Budget Totals in Billions of Dollars:														
Receipts	3,330	3,438	3,645	3,877	4,129	4,421	4,753	5,040	5,323	5,608	5,939	6,292	20,824	49,027
Outlays	4,109	4,529	4,746	4,945	5,177	5,330	5,453	5,671	5,899	6,122	6,447	6,495	25,651	56,286
Deficit	779	1,092	1,101	1,068	1,049	909	700	631	577	513	508	202	4,827	7,259
Debt held by the public	15,750	16,919	18,087	19,222	20,334	21,304	22,064	22,756	23,390	23,957	24,519	24,770		
Gross domestic product (GDP)	20,236	21,289	22,410	23,558	24,753	26,007	27,326	28,700	30,116	31,580	33,116	34,727		
Budget Totals as a Percent of GDP:														
Receipts	16.5%	16.1%	16.3%	16.5%	16.7%	17.0%	17.4%	17.6%	17.7%	17.8%	17.9%	18.1%	16.8%	17.3%
Outlays	20.3%	21.3%	21.2%	21.0%	20.9%	20.5%	20.0%	19.8%	19.6%	19.4%	19.5%	18.7%	20.7%	20.0%
Deficit	3.8%	5.1%	4.9%	4.5%	4.2%	3.5%	2.6%	2.2%	1.9%	1.6%	1.5%	0.6%	3.9%	2.8%
Debt held by the public	77.8%	79.5%	80.7%	81.6%	82.1%	81.9%	80.7%	79.3%	77.7%	75.9%	74.0%	71.3%		

Table S–2. Effect of Budget Proposals on Projected Deficits

(Deficit increases (+) or decreases (–) in billions of dollars)

	2018	2019	2020	2021	2022	2023	2024	2025	2026	2027	2028	2029	Totals 2020–2024	Totals 2020–2029
Projected deficits in the baseline	**779**	**1,098**	**1,067**	**1,049**	**1,102**	**1,019**	**891**	**937**	**984**	**1,000**	**1,125**	**927**	**5,128**	**10,100**
Percent of GDP	3.9%	5.2%	4.8%	4.5%	4.5%	3.9%	3.3%	3.3%	3.3%	3.2%	3.4%	2.7%		
Proposals in the 2020 Budget:														
Invest in critical national priorities:														
Provide defense funding to rebuild and restore the military and protect the Nation	....	....	55	76	83	79	74	51	37	25	17	13	367	510
Implement the VA MISSION Act of 2018	....	....	8	10	10	10	10	10	10	10	10	10	49	99
Support major investment in infrastructure	....	....	5	26	40	50	40	19	10	5	5	0	160	199
Establish Education Freedom Scholarships	....	....	1	5	5	5	5	5	5	5	5	5	21	45
Provide paid parental leave	....	....	1	1	1	2	2	2	3	3	3	3	7	20
Debt service	....	....	1	4	9	14	18	22	25	28	30	32	46	183
Total	....	....	**71**	**122**	**148**	**159**	**149**	**110**	**89**	**76**	**70**	**63**	**650**	**1,058**
Restrain spending to protect and respect American taxpayers:														
Right-size Government and apply two-penny plan to non-defense discretionary spending	....	....	23	–8	–46	–72	–99	–127	–154	–181	–207	–233	–202	–1,105
Empowering States and consumers to reform healthcare	....	....	4	14	–27	–40	–57	–75	–86	–107	–130	–154	–106	–659
Address wasteful spending, fraud, and abuse in healthcare	....	....	–10	–24	–32	–39	–45	–52	–64	–70	–77	–83	–151	–496
Improve drug pricing and payment policies	....	....	–0	–3	–4	–6	–7	–9	–9	–10	–11	–11	–20	–69
Improve the welfare system	....	....	–22	–30	–32	–33	–34	–34	–35	–35	–35	–36	–151	–327
Reform Federal student loans	....	....	–6	–11	–16	–20	–22	–24	–25	–27	–28	–28	–75	–207
Reform disability programs and test new approaches	....	....	–1	–2	–2	–3	–4	–7	–10	–14	–19	–23	–11	–84
Modify retirement and health benefits for Federal employees	....	....	–5	–3	–6	–7	–9	–11	–13	–14	–16	–17	–31	–102
Implement agricultural reforms	....	....	–2	–5	–6	–7	–7	–7	–7	–7	–7	–7	–26	–61
Reform the Postal Service	....	....	–4	–8	–8	–9	–10	–10	–11	–12	–13	–13	–39	–98
Other spending reductions and program reforms	....	–6	–12	–18	–14	–19	–21	–23	–30	–18	–57	–72	–84	–285
Debt service and other interest effects	....	–*	–1	–3	–8	–16	–25	–37	–51	–68	–87	–110	–53	–406
Total	....	**–6**	**–37**	**–103**	**–201**	**–270**	**–340**	**–416**	**–496**	**–563**	**–687**	**–788**	**–950**	**–3,899**
Total proposals in the 2020 Budget	....	**–6**	**34**	**19**	**–53**	**–110**	**–191**	**–306**	**–407**	**–487**	**–617**	**–724**	**–301**	**–2,841**
Resulting deficits in the 2020 Budget	**779**	**1,092**	**1,101**	**1,068**	**1,049**	**909**	**700**	**631**	**577**	**513**	**508**	**202**	**4,827**	**7,259**
Percent of GDP	3.8%	5.1%	4.9%	4.5%	4.2%	3.5%	2.6%	2.2%	1.9%	1.6%	1.5%	0.6%		

* $500 million or less.

Table S–3. Baseline by Category [1]

(In billions of dollars)

	2018	2019	2020	2021	2022	2023	2024	2025	2026	2027	2028	2029	Totals 2020–2024	Totals 2020–2029
Outlays:														
Discretionary programs:														
Defense	623	674	671	674	674	686	698	712	731	749	767	787	3,403	7,149
Non-defense	639	685	669	654	658	662	672	682	697	712	727	743	3,316	6,877
Subtotal, discretionary programs	1,262	1,359	1,340	1,328	1,332	1,348	1,371	1,394	1,427	1,461	1,494	1,530	6,719	14,026
Mandatory programs:														
Social Security	982	1,041	1,102	1,166	1,235	1,309	1,387	1,468	1,553	1,642	1,737	1,835	6,199	14,434
Medicare	582	645	702	762	861	892	920	1,038	1,121	1,202	1,385	1,361	4,136	10,244
Medicaid	389	419	426	446	470	499	525	554	593	628	664	703	2,365	5,508
Exchange subsidies (including Basic Health Program)	46	56	50	50	52	53	55	57	58	61	63	66	260	565
Other mandatory programs	523	622	607	623	666	666	668	703	747	771	836	804	3,231	7,092
Subtotal, mandatory programs	2,522	2,783	2,887	3,047	3,284	3,419	3,554	3,821	4,073	4,304	4,685	4,769	16,191	37,843
Net interest	325	394	482	548	611	666	709	749	789	828	868	903	3,018	7,154
Total outlays	4,109	4,536	4,709	4,923	5,228	5,434	5,634	5,963	6,290	6,593	7,048	7,202	25,927	59,022
Receipts:														
Individual income taxes	1,684	1,698	1,822	1,946	2,081	2,236	2,392	2,564	2,748	2,939	3,146	3,359	10,476	25,231
Corporation income taxes	205	216	256	284	314	370	418	443	428	418	428	432	1,642	3,791
Social insurance and retirement receipts:														
Social Security payroll taxes	855	911	949	1,004	1,059	1,114	1,175	1,236	1,306	1,372	1,456	1,531	5,301	12,202
Medicare payroll taxes	261	276	289	307	325	343	362	382	404	425	452	476	1,626	3,764
Unemployment insurance	45	44	46	46	46	46	47	49	50	52	54	56	231	492
Other retirement	10	11	11	12	12	13	13	14	15	15	16	17	61	139
Excise taxes	95	99	108	111	114	107	136	126	130	133	122	142	576	1,229
Estate and gift taxes	23	19	19	20	22	23	25	27	28	29	31	32	110	256
Customs duties	41	69	48	45	48	51	54	57	60	63	66	69	247	559
Deposits of earnings, Federal Reserve System	71	49	49	52	56	62	68	73	79	84	90	97	288	711
Other miscellaneous receipts	41	44	44	47	48	50	53	57	60	61	63	65	242	548
Total receipts	3,330	3,438	3,643	3,874	4,126	4,415	4,742	5,026	5,306	5,592	5,923	6,275	20,800	48,922
Deficit	**779**	**1,098**	**1,067**	**1,049**	**1,102**	**1,019**	**891**	**937**	**984**	**1,000**	**1,125**	**927**	**5,128**	**10,100**
Net interest	325	394	482	548	611	666	709	749	789	828	868	903	3,018	7,154
Primary deficit	454	704	584	501	490	353	182	188	195	172	257	24	2,110	2,946
On-budget deficit	785	1,100	1,047	1,021	1,062	965	823	854	898	903	1,024	809	4,918	9,404
Off-budget deficit/surplus (–)	–6	–2	20	28	40	54	68	83	86	98	101	118	210	696
Memorandum, budget authority for discretionary programs:														
Defense	701	716	647	662	679	695	712	730	748	766	785	805	3,395	7,229
Non-defense	722	621	567	581	595	610	625	641	657	673	690	707	2,978	6,346
Total, discretionary budget authority	1,423	1,337	1,214	1,243	1,274	1,305	1,337	1,371	1,405	1,439	1,475	1,512	6,373	13,575

[1] Baseline estimates are on the basis of the economic assumptions shown in Table S–9, which incorporate the effects of the Administration's fiscal policies.

Table S–4. Proposed Budget by Category

(In billions of dollars)

	2018	2019	2020	2021	2022	2023	2024	2025	2026	2027	2028	2029	Totals 2020-2024	Totals 2020-2029
Outlays:														
Discretionary programs:														
Defense	623	674	726	750	757	765	773	763	767	774	785	799	3,770	7,659
Non-defense	639	685	700	651	616	592	574	555	542	531	520	511	3,131	5,790
Subtotal, discretionary programs	1,262	1,359	1,426	1,400	1,373	1,356	1,346	1,319	1,309	1,305	1,305	1,310	6,901	13,449
Mandatory programs:														
Social Security	982	1,041	1,102	1,165	1,234	1,307	1,384	1,465	1,550	1,638	1,733	1,831	6,192	14,408
Medicare	582	645	679	711	800	822	840	949	1,025	1,109	1,251	1,212	3,851	9,398
Medicaid and Market-Based Health Care Grant	389	419	418	491	483	502	512	527	550	567	585	602	2,406	5,237
Exchange subsidies (including Basic Health Program)	46	56	50	9	....	....	....	....	....	....	....	....	59	59
Other mandatory programs	523	615	587	595	638	630	629	659	693	710	759	716	3,079	6,617
Allowance for infrastructure initiative	....	....	5	26	40	50	40	19	10	5	5	*	160	199
Subtotal, mandatory programs	2,522	2,777	2,841	2,997	3,195	3,310	3,405	3,619	3,828	4,029	4,333	4,361	15,748	35,919
Net interest	325	393	479	548	610	664	702	733	762	788	810	823	3,002	6,918
Total outlays	4,109	4,529	4,746	4,945	5,177	5,330	5,453	5,671	5,899	6,122	6,447	6,495	25,651	56,286
Receipts:														
Individual income taxes	1,684	1,698	1,824	1,946	2,081	2,237	2,394	2,568	2,752	2,944	3,151	3,365	10,482	25,263
Corporation income taxes	205	216	255	284	315	371	418	443	429	418	428	432	1,643	3,794
Social insurance and retirement receipts:														
Social Security payroll taxes	855	911	949	1,003	1,059	1,113	1,174	1,235	1,305	1,371	1,455	1,530	5,299	12,194
Medicare payroll taxes	261	276	289	307	325	343	362	381	403	425	451	476	1,625	3,762
Unemployment insurance	45	44	46	46	47	48	49	52	54	54	56	58	236	510
Other retirement	10	11	11	14	17	19	22	24	26	27	28	29	83	217
Excise taxes	95	99	109	111	115	108	136	127	130	134	123	143	579	1,236
Estate and gift taxes	23	19	19	20	22	23	25	27	28	29	31	32	110	256
Customs duties	41	69	48	45	48	51	54	57	60	63	66	69	247	559
Deposits of earnings, Federal Reserve System	71	49	49	53	57	62	69	74	79	85	91	97	290	717
Other miscellaneous receipts	41	44	45	47	48	50	53	57	60	62	64	65	243	550
Allowance for empowering States and consumers to reform healthcare	....	....	–1	*	–3	–4	–4	–4	–4	–3	–4	–4	–13	–32
Total receipts	3,330	3,438	3,645	3,877	4,129	4,421	4,753	5,040	5,323	5,608	5,939	6,292	20,824	49,027
Deficit	**779**	**1,092**	**1,101**	**1,068**	**1,049**	**909**	**700**	**631**	**577**	**513**	**508**	**202**	**4,827**	**7,259**
Net interest	325	393	479	548	610	664	702	733	762	788	810	823	3,002	6,918
Primary deficit/surplus (–)	454	698	622	521	439	245	–1	–102	–185	–274	–301	–621	1,825	341
On-budget deficit	785	1,094	1,082	1,043	1,012	857	635	552	496	422	414	91	4,630	6,604
Off-budget deficit/surplus (–)	–6	–2	18	25	36	51	65	79	81	91	94	111	197	654

Table S–4. Proposed Budget by Category—Continued

(In billions of dollars)

	2018	2019	2020	2021	2022	2023	2024	2025	2026	2027	2028	2029	Totals 2020-2024	Totals 2020-2029
Memorandum, budget authority for discretionary programs:														
Defense	701	716	750	746	760	778	784	752	768	784	800	817	3,818	7,739
Non-defense	722	621	563	538	527	517	506	495	485	475	466	458	2,650	5,028
Total, discretionary budget authority	1,423	1,337	1,313	1,284	1,287	1,295	1,290	1,247	1,253	1,259	1,266	1,275	6,468	12,767
Memorandum, empowering States and consumers to reform healthcare–Medicaid and other outlays for healthcare coverage:														
Medicaid	389	419	418	368	357	374	381	392	413	427	441	455	1,898	4,025
Exchange Subsidies (including Basic Health Program)	46	56	50	9	....	....	....	....	....	....	....	....	59	59
Market-Based Health Care Grant	....	....	....	123	126	128	131	134	138	141	144	147	508	1,212
Total, outlays	435	475	468	500	483	502	512	527	550	567	585	602	2,465	5,296

* $500 million or less.

Table S–5. Proposed Budget by Category as a Percent of GDP

(As a percent of GDP)

	2018	2019	2020	2021	2022	2023	2024	2025	2026	2027	2028	2029	Averages 2020–2024	Averages 2020–2029
Outlays:														
Discretionary programs:														
Defense	3.1	3.2	3.2	3.2	3.1	2.9	2.8	2.7	2.5	2.5	2.4	2.3	3.0	2.8
Non-defense	3.2	3.2	3.1	2.8	2.5	2.3	2.1	1.9	1.8	1.7	1.6	1.5	2.5	2.1
Subtotal, discretionary programs	6.2	6.4	6.4	5.9	5.5	5.2	4.9	4.6	4.3	4.1	3.9	3.8	5.6	4.9
Mandatory programs:														
Social Security	4.9	4.9	4.9	4.9	5.0	5.0	5.1	5.1	5.1	5.2	5.2	5.3	5.0	5.1
Medicare	2.9	3.0	3.0	3.0	3.2	3.2	3.1	3.3	3.4	3.5	3.8	3.5	3.1	3.3
Medicaid and Market-Based Health Care Grant	1.9	2.0	1.9	2.1	2.0	1.9	1.9	1.8	1.8	1.8	1.8	1.7	1.9	1.9
Exchange subsidies (including Basic Health Program)	0.2	0.3	0.2	*	....	....	....	....	....	....	....	....	0.1	*
Other mandatory programs	2.6	2.9	2.6	2.5	2.6	2.4	2.3	2.3	2.3	2.2	2.3	2.1	2.5	2.4
Allowance for infrastructure initiative	....	....	*	0.1	0.2	0.2	0.1	0.1	*	*	*	*	0.1	0.1
Subtotal, mandatory programs	12.5	13.0	12.7	12.7	12.9	12.7	12.5	12.6	12.7	12.8	13.1	12.6	12.7	12.7
Net interest	1.6	1.8	2.1	2.3	2.5	2.6	2.6	2.6	2.5	2.5	2.4	2.4	2.4	2.4
Total outlays	20.3	21.3	21.2	21.0	20.9	20.5	20.0	19.8	19.6	19.4	19.5	18.7	20.7	20.0
Receipts:														
Individual income taxes	8.3	8.0	8.1	8.3	8.4	8.6	8.8	8.9	9.1	9.3	9.5	9.7	8.4	8.9
Corporation income taxes	1.0	1.0	1.1	1.2	1.3	1.4	1.5	1.5	1.4	1.3	1.3	1.2	1.3	1.3
Social insurance and retirement receipts:														
Social Security payroll taxes	4.2	4.3	4.2	4.3	4.3	4.3	4.3	4.3	4.3	4.3	4.4	4.4	4.3	4.3
Medicare payroll taxes	1.3	1.3	1.3	1.3	1.3	1.3	1.3	1.3	1.3	1.3	1.4	1.4	1.3	1.3
Unemployment insurance	0.2	0.2	0.2	0.2	0.2	0.2	0.2	0.2	0.2	0.2	0.2	0.2	0.2	0.2
Other retirement	0.1	0.1	*	0.1	0.1	0.1	0.1	0.1	0.1	0.1	0.1	0.1	0.1	0.1
Excise taxes	0.5	0.5	0.5	0.5	0.5	0.4	0.5	0.4	0.4	0.4	0.4	0.4	0.5	0.4
Estate and gift taxes	0.1	0.1	0.1	0.1	0.1	0.1	0.1	0.1	0.1	0.1	0.1	0.1	0.1	0.1
Customs duties	0.2	0.3	0.2	0.2	0.2	0.2	0.2	0.2	0.2	0.2	0.2	0.2	0.2	0.2
Deposits of earnings, Federal Reserve System	0.3	0.2	0.2	0.2	0.2	0.2	0.3	0.3	0.3	0.3	0.3	0.3	0.2	0.3
Other miscellaneous receipts	0.2	0.2	0.2	0.2	0.2	0.2	0.2	0.2	0.2	0.2	0.2	0.2	0.2	0.2
Allowance for empowering States and consumers to reform healthcare	....	....	–*	*	–*	–*	–*	–*	–*	–*	–*	–*	–*	–*
Total receipts	16.5	16.1	16.3	16.5	16.7	17.0	17.4	17.6	17.7	17.8	17.9	18.1	16.8	17.3
Deficit	**3.8**	**5.1**	**4.9**	**4.5**	**4.2**	**3.5**	**2.6**	**2.2**	**1.9**	**1.6**	**1.5**	**0.6**	**3.9**	**2.8**
Net interest	1.6	1.8	2.1	2.3	2.5	2.6	2.6	2.6	2.5	2.5	2.4	2.4	2.4	2.4
Primary deficit/surplus (–)	2.2	3.3	2.8	2.2	1.8	0.9	–*	–0.4	–0.6	–0.9	–0.9	–1.8	1.5	0.3
On-budget deficit	3.9	5.1	4.8	4.4	4.1	3.3	2.3	1.9	1.6	1.3	1.3	0.3	3.8	2.5
Off-budget deficit/surplus (–)	–*	–*	0.1	0.1	0.1	0.2	0.2	0.3	0.3	0.3	0.3	0.3	0.2	0.2

Table S–5. Proposed Budget by Category as a Percent of GDP—Continued

(As a percent of GDP)

	2018	2019	2020	2021	2022	2023	2024	2025	2026	2027	2028	2029	Averages 2020–2024	Averages 2020–2029
Memorandum, budget authority for discretionary programs:														
Defense	3.5	3.4	3.3	3.2	3.1	3.0	2.9	2.6	2.6	2.5	2.4	2.4	3.1	2.8
Non-defense	3.6	2.9	2.5	2.3	2.1	2.0	1.9	1.7	1.6	1.5	1.4	1.3	2.2	1.8
Total, discretionary budget authority	7.0	6.3	5.9	5.5	5.2	5.0	4.7	4.3	4.2	4.0	3.8	3.7	5.2	4.6
Memorandum, empowering States and consumers to reform healthcare–Medicaid and other outlays for healthcare coverage:														
Medicaid	1.9	2.0	1.9	1.6	1.4	1.4	1.4	1.4	1.4	1.4	1.3	1.3	1.5	1.4
Exchange Subsidies (including Basic Health Program)	0.2	0.3	0.2	*	....	....	....	....	....	....	....	....	0.1	*
Market-Based Health Care Grant	....	....	....	0.5	0.5	0.5	0.5	0.5	0.5	0.4	0.4	0.4	0.4	0.4
Total, outlays	2.2	2.2	2.1	2.1	2.0	1.9	1.9	1.8	1.8	1.8	1.8	1.7	2.0	1.9

*0.05 percent of GDP or less.

Table S–6. Mandatory and Receipt Proposals

(Deficit increases (+) or decreases (–) in millions of dollars)

	2019	2020	2021	2022	2023	2024	2025	2026	2027	2028	2029	Totals 2020–2024	Totals 2020–2029
Mandatory Initiatives and Savings:													
Agriculture:													
Establish Food Safety and Inspection Service (FSIS) user fee	....	....	–660	–660	–660	–660	–660	–660	–660	–660	–660	–2,640	–5,940
Establish Animal and Plant Health Inspection Service user fee	....	–22	–22	–23	–23	–24	–24	–24	–25	–25	–26	–114	–238
Establish Packers and Stockyards Program user fee	....	–25	–25	–25	–25	–25	–25	–25	–25	–25	–25	–125	–250
Establish Agricultural Marketing Service user fee	....	–20	–20	–20	–20	–20	–20	–20	–20	–20	–20	–100	–200
Adjust FSIS holiday and voluntary overtime user fee	....	....	....	....	....	....	....	....	....	....	....	....	....
Eliminate the Rural Economic Development program	....	....	....	–5	–5	....	....	....	....	....	....	–10	–10
Improve Child Nutrition program integrity	....	–19	–124	–155	–188	–193	–198	–203	–208	–213	–218	–679	–1,719
Reform commodity purchases under Section 32	....	–411	–432	–454	–476	–499	–523	–547	–571	–596	–621	–2,272	–5,130
Establish Forest Service Mineral Program cost recovery fee	....	–29	–14	1	1	1	1	1	1	1	1	–40	–35
Amend land uses cost recovery authority	....	–2	–1	....	....	....	....	....	....	....	....	–3	–3
Limit eligibility for agricultural commodity payments to $500,000 Adjusted Gross Income (AGI)	....	–63	–117	–132	–124	–114	–126	–154	–148	–164	–164	–550	–1,306
Streamline conservation programs	....	–210	–412	–617	–838	–1,040	–1,081	–1,131	–1,181	–1,181	–1,181	–3,117	–8,872
Eliminate lower priority Farm Bill programs	....	–54	–86	–97	–99	–100	–100	–100	–100	–100	–100	–436	–936
Eliminate Food for Progress food aid program	....	–166	–166	–166	–166	–166	–166	–166	–166	–166	–166	–830	–1,660
Tighten commodity payment limits and close loopholes	....	–149	–143	–141	–137	–135	–132	–130	–128	–127	–126	–705	–1,348
Eliminate Livestock Forage program	....	–680	–778	–769	–759	–758	–791	–815	–817	–827	–825	–3,744	–7,819
Eliminate the crop insurance 508(h) program	....	–12	–12	–12	–12	–12	–12	–12	–12	–12	–12	–60	–120
Limit Crop Insurance eligibility to $500,000 AGI	....	....	–62	–69	–69	–68	–69	–68	–69	–78	–89	–268	–641
Reduce Crop Insurance premium subsidies	....	....	–2,253	–2,321	–2,507	–2,488	–2,497	–2,482	–2,504	–2,522	–2,542	–9,569	–22,116
Cap Crop Insurance companies' underwriting gains	....	....	....	....	–417	–428	–423	–419	–421	–418	–422	–845	–2,948
Total, Agriculture	....	–1,862	–5,327	–5,665	–6,524	–6,729	–6,846	–6,955	–7,054	–7,133	–7,196	–26,107	–61,291
Commerce:													
Lease Shared Secondary Licenses	....	–40	–35	–35	–60	–65	–70	–70	–80	–80	–85	–235	–620

Table S–6. Mandatory and Receipt Proposals—Continued

(Deficit increases (+) or decreases (–) in millions of dollars)

	2019	2020	2021	2022	2023	2024	2025	2026	2027	2028	2029	Totals 2020–2024	Totals 2020–2029
Education:													
Reform Federal student loans:													
Create single income-driven student loan repayment plan:													
Create single income-driven student loan repayment plan [2]	....	–1,343	–3,077	–4,725	–6,324	–7,643	–8,643	–9,129	–9,999	–10,511	–11,274	–23,112	–72,668
Eliminate standard repayment cap	....	–1,857	–3,232	–4,376	–5,220	–5,840	–6,227	–6,411	–6,563	–6,568	–6,422	–20,525	–52,716
Use combined AGI to calculate loan payments for married filing separately	....	–95	–170	–255	–326	–400	–445	–457	–505	–538	–580	–1,246	–3,771
Total, create single income-driven student loan repayment plan	....	–3,295	–6,479	–9,356	–11,870	–13,883	–15,315	–15,997	–17,067	–17,617	–18,276	–44,883	–129,155
Eliminate subsidized student loans	....	–659	–2,094	–2,471	–2,660	–2,726	–2,709	–2,768	–2,769	–2,724	–2,767	–10,610	–24,347
Eliminate Public Service Loan Forgiveness	....	–1,459	–2,842	–4,015	–4,975	–5,688	–6,226	–6,477	–6,819	–7,231	–7,281	–18,979	–53,013
Eliminate account maintenance fee payments to guaranty agencies	....	–501	....	....	....	....	....	....	....	....	....	–501	–501
Enact student loan risk sharing	....	....	....	....	....	....	....	....	....	....	....	....	....
Total, Reform Federal student loans	....	–5,914	–11,415	–15,842	–19,505	–22,297	–24,250	–25,242	–26,655	–27,572	–28,324	–74,973	–207,016
Establish Education Freedom Scholarships [1]	....	893	4,847	4,928	5,006	4,974	5,036	4,916	4,934	4,960	4,994	20,648	45,488
Reduce improper payments in Pell Grants	....	–10	–21	–22	–22	–22	–23	–23	–24	–24	–24	–97	–215
Move Iraq-Afghanistan Service Grants into the Pell Grant program	....	....	....	....	....	....	....	....	....	....	....	....	....
Expand Pell Grants to short-term programs	....	12	30	35	42	47	47	49	50	52	52	166	416
Reallocate mandatory Pell funding to support short-term programs	....	–12	–30	–35	–42	–47	–47	–49	–50	–52	–52	–166	–416
Total, Education	....	–5,031	–6,589	–10,936	–14,521	–17,345	–19,237	–20,349	–21,745	–22,636	–23,354	–54,422	–161,743
Energy:													
Repeal borrowing authority for Western Area Power Administration (WAPA)	....	–550	–615	455	–5	425	–225	225	–225	225	–225	–290	–515
Divest WAPA transmission assets	....	....	–847	....	....	....	....	....	....	....	....	–847	–847
Divest Southwestern Power Administration transmission assets	....	....	–16	....	....	....	....	....	....	....	....	–16	–16
Divest Bonneville Power Administration transmission assets	....	....	–2,334	–396	–414	–432	–395	–427	–438	–448	–459	–3,576	–5,743
Reform the laws governing how Power Marketing Administrations establish power rates	....	–247	–253	–259	–266	–274	–283	–291	–298	–304	–268	–1,299	–2,743
Restart Nuclear Waste Fund Fee in 2022	....	....	....	–355	–354	–353	–345	–337	–337	–337	–337	–1,062	–2,755
Total, Energy	....	–797	–4,065	–555	–1,039	–634	–1,248	–830	–1,298	–864	–1,289	–7,090	–12,619

Table S–6. Mandatory and Receipt Proposals—Continued

(Deficit increases (+) or decreases (–) in millions of dollars)

	2019	2020	2021	2022	2023	2024	2025	2026	2027	2028	2029	Totals 2020–2024	Totals 2020–2029
Health and Human Services (HHS):													
Create child welfare flexible funding option	....	....	....	....	....	....	....	....	....	....	....	....	....
Expand the Regional Partnership Grants program	....	11	34	38	39	40	40	40	42	42	42	162	368
Reauthorize Personal Responsibility Education Program and Sexual Risk Avoidance education	....	5	80	53	8	2	....	....	....	....	....	148	148
Reauthorize Health Profession Opportunity Grants	....	3	45	18	13	4	2	....	....	....	....	83	85
Mitigate Impact of Temporary Assistance for Needy Families (TANF) and Social-Services Block Grant (SSBG) program changes on child care spending	....	216	216	216	216	216	215	215	215	215	215	1,080	2,155
Expand Access to National Directory of New Hires	....	....	....	....	....	....	....	....	....	....	....	....	....
Reauthorize Healthy Marriage and Responsible Fatherhood Grants	....	....	....	....	....	....	....	....	....	....	....	....	....
Fund States to provide parenting time services	....	2	2	2	3	3	4	4	5	5	5	12	35
Modernize and expand the Court Improvement Program	....	9	26	30	30	30	30	30	31	35	29	125	280
Promote family based care	....	14	18	32	36	41	47	43	42	42	42	141	357
Increase repatriation ceiling	....	....	1	1	1	1	1	1	1	1	1	4	9
Build the supply of child care	....	50	300	300	300	50	....	....	....	....	....	1,000	1,000
Establish an Unaccompanied Alien Children Contingency Fund	....	480	221	22	7	4	4	....	....	....	....	734	738
Create Child and Family Services review incentives	....	....	....	7	8	8	8	21	22	18	18	23	110
Drug pricing and payment improvements:													
Public Health:													
Improve 340B program integrity	....	....	....	....	....	....	....	....	....	....	....	....	....
Establish and collect user fees from the 340B drug discount program from participating covered entities	....	....	....	....	....	....	....	....	....	....	....	....	....
Reform exclusivity for first generics to spur greater competition and access	....	–75	–85	–95	–100	–100	–120	–130	–145	–165	–145	–455	–1,160
Reform 180-day exclusivity forfeiture provision for first generics to increase competition[3]	....	....	....	....	....	....	....	....	....	....	....	....	....
Enhance Food and Drug Administration (FDA) authority to address abuse of petition process[3]	....	....	....	....	....	....	....	....	....	....	....	....	....

Table S–6. Mandatory and Receipt Proposals—Continued

(Deficit increases (+) or decreases (–) in millions of dollars)

	2019	2020	2021	2022	2023	2024	2025	2026	2027	2028	2029	Totals 2020–2024	Totals 2020–2029
Revise United States Pharmacopeia compendial requirements for biological products to encourage biosimilar development [3]	....	....	....	....	....	....	....	....	....	....	....	....	....
Codify FDA's approach to determining new chemical entity exclusivity [3]	....	....	....	....	....	....	....	....	....	....	....	....	....
Total, public health	....	–75	–85	–95	–100	–100	–120	–130	–145	–165	–145	–455	–1,160
Medicare:													
Eliminate cost-sharing on generic drugs and biosimilars for low-income beneficiaries	....	....	–70	–90	–100	–90	–90	–110	–110	–130	–140	–350	–930
Exclude manufacturer discounts from the calculation of beneficiary out-of-pocket costs in the Medicare Part D coverage gap	....	....	–3,120	–5,260	–6,830	–8,230	–9,860	–9,170	–9,910	–11,590	–10,760	–23,440	–74,730
Establish a beneficiary out-of-pocket maximum in the Medicare Part D catastrophic phase	....	....	780	1,860	1,930	1,740	1,620	1,220	1,450	2,210	1,220	6,310	14,030
Give the Secretary authority to contract with pharmaceutical manufacturers entering into new coverage gap discount program agreements on a quarterly basis [3]	....	....	....	....	....	....	....	....	....	....	....	....	....
Permanently authorize a successful pilot on retroactive Medicare Part D coverage for low-income beneficiaries	....	–20	–20	–20	–30	–30	–30	–30	–40	–40	–40	–120	–300
Authorize the HHS Secretary to leverage Medicare Part D plans' negotiating power for certain drugs covered under Part B [3]	....	....	....	....	....	....	....	....	....	....	....	....	....
Address abusive drug pricing by manufacturers by establishing an inflation limit for reimbursement of Medicare Part B drugs [3]	....	....	....	....	....	....	....	....	....	....	....	....	....
Improve manufacturers' reporting of average sales prices to set accurate payment rates [3]	....	....	....	....	....	....	....	....	....	....	....	....	....
Modify payment for drugs hospitals purchased through the 340B discount program and require a minimum level of charity care for hospitals to receive a payment adjustment related to uncompensated care [3]	....	....	....	....	....	....	....	....	....	....	....	....	....
Eliminate pass-through payments for drugs, biologicals, and biosimilars	....	–150	–280	–320	–350	–400	–440	–490	–550	–610	–680	–1,500	–4,270

Table S–6. Mandatory and Receipt Proposals—Continued

(Deficit increases (+) or decreases (–) in millions of dollars)

	2019	2020	2021	2022	2023	2024	2025	2026	2027	2028	2029	Totals 2020–2024	Totals 2020–2029
Reduce Wholesale Acquisition Cost-based payments [3]	....	....	....	....	....	....	....	....	....	....	....	....	....
Reduce average sales price-based payments when the primary patent expires to increase competition and reduce gaming [3]	....	....	....	....	....	....	....	....	....	....	....	....	....
Total, Medicare	....	–170	–2,710	–3,830	–5,380	–7,010	–8,800	–8,580	–9,160	–10,160	–10,400	–19,100	–66,200
Medicaid:													
Clarify authorized generic sales under the Medicaid Drug Rebate program	....	–15	–15	–15	–15	–15	–15	–15	–15	–15	–15	–75	–150
Test allowing State Medicaid programs to negotiate prices directly with drug manufacturers and set formulary for coverage	....	–5	–15	–25	–35	–40	–45	–50	–60	–65	–70	–120	–410
Impose greater penalties for manufacturer reporting of false information or false product data under the Medicaid Drug Rebate Program [3]	....	....	....	....	....	....	....	....	....	....	....	....	....
Exclude brand name and authorized generic drug prices from Medicaid Federal upper limit	....	–90	–90	–100	–100	–100	–100	–100	–100	–100	–100	–480	–980
Clarify definitions under the Medicaid Drug Rebate Program to prevent inappropriately low manufacturer rebates	....	–26	–26	–27	–32	–32	–37	–38	–38	–43	–48	–143	–347
Allow rebates on drugs that exceed 100 percent of the Average Manufacturer Price [3]	....	....	....	....	....	....	....	....	....	....	....	....	....
Total, Medicaid	....	–136	–146	–167	–182	–187	–197	–203	–213	–223	–233	–818	–1,887
Total, drug pricing and payment improvements	....	–381	–2,941	–4,092	–5,662	–7,297	–9,117	–8,913	–9,518	–10,548	–10,778	–20,373	–69,247
Address opioids:													
Prevent abusive prescribing by establishing HHS reciprocity with the Drug Enforcement Administration to terminate provider prescribing authority [3]	....	....	....	....	....	....	....	....	....	....	....	....	....
Allow States to extend Medicaid coverage for pregnant women with substance use disorder to one year postpartum	....	25	20	25	25	25	25	25	25	25	25	120	245
Total, address opioids	....	25	20	25	25	25	25	25	25	25	25	120	245
Medicare Appeals:													
Improve the Medicare appeals system	....	....	....	....	....	....	....	....	....	....	....	....	....

Table S–6. Mandatory and Receipt Proposals—Continued

(Deficit increases (+) or decreases (–) in millions of dollars)

	2019	2020	2021	2022	2023	2024	2025	2026	2027	2028	2029	Totals 2020–2024	Totals 2020–2029
Address wasteful spending, fraud, and abuse in Medicare:													
Improve and tailor the way Medicare educates beneficiaries about the program	....	40	60	70	70	70	70	70	70	80	80	310	680
Eliminate arbitrary thresholds and other burdens to encourage participation in advanced Alternative Payment Models [3]	....	–350	–350	–240	100	220	60	20	50	90	120	–620	–280
Simplify and eliminate reporting burdens for clinicians participating in the Merit-based Incentive Payment System	....	....	....	....	....	....	....	....	....	....	....	....	....
Tailor the frequency of skilled nursing facility surveys to more efficiently use resources and alleviate burden for top-performing nursing homes	....	....	....	....	....	....	....	....	....	....	....	....	....
Remove timeframe for initial surveys for End Stage Renal Disease facilities under the Bipartisan Budget Act of 2018	....	....	....	....	....	....	....	....	....	....	....	....	....
Allow Centers for Medicare and Medicaid Services (CMS) flexibility to determine the frequency of Programs of All-Inclusive Care for the Elderly program audits	....	....	....	....	....	....	....	....	....	....	....	....	....
Eliminate the unnecessary requirement of a face-to-face provider visit for durable medical equipment	....	....	....	....	....	....	....	....	....	....	....	....	....
Remove the redundant requirement that physicians certify that all critical access hospital patients are expected to be discharged within 96 hours of admission	....	....	....	....	....	....	....	....	....	....	....	....	....
Create a consolidated hospital quality payment program	....	....	....	....	....	....	....	....	....	....	....	....	....
Authorize the Secretary to implement meaningful measures for the End Stage Renal Disease Quality Incentive Program	....	....	....	....	....	....	....	....	....	....	....	....	....
Increase End Stage Renal Disease networks funding to match Consumer Price Index [3]	....	....	....	....	....	....	....	....	....	....	....	....	....
Consolidate and block grant graduate medical education payments	....	–790	–1,240	–2,110	–3,090	–4,030	–5,110	–6,120	–7,220	–8,440	–9,710	–11,260	–47,860
Modify payments to hospitals for uncompensated care	....	....	–6,030	–7,540	–8,620	–9,670	–10,780	–11,940	–13,180	–14,460	–15,790	–31,860	–98,010
Reduce Medicare coverage of bad debts	....	–410	–1,390	–2,940	–3,920	–4,250	–4,520	–4,810	–5,100	–5,420	–5,750	–12,910	–38,510

Table S–6. Mandatory and Receipt Proposals—Continued

(Deficit increases (+) or decreases (–) in millions of dollars)

	2019	2020	2021	2022	2023	2024	2025	2026	2027	2028	2029	Totals 2020–2024	Totals 2020–2029
Address excessive payment for post-acute care providers by establishing a unified payment system based on patients' clinical needs rather than the site of care	....	–1,210	–2,880	–5,000	–7,670	–10,470	–12,280	–13,440	–14,700	–16,570	–16,930	–27,230	–101,150
Authorize long-term care hospital site neutral exceptions criteria	....	–530	–820	–890	–950	–1,000	–1,060	–1,120	–1,150	–1,210	–1,270	–4,190	–10,000
Pay all hospital-owned physician offices located off-campus at the physician office rate	....	–1,100	–2,010	–2,220	–2,460	–2,720	–2,990	–3,280	–3,600	–3,940	–4,340	–10,510	–28,660
Pay on-campus hospital outpatient departments at the physician office rate for certain services	....	–4,670	–8,600	–9,670	–10,870	–12,170	–13,580	–15,170	–16,940	–18,840	–20,890	–45,980	–131,400
Redesign Outpatient Prospective Payment System and Ambulatory Surgical Center payment systems to make risk-adjusted payments [3]	....	....	....	....	....	....	....	....	....	....	....	....	....
Implement value-based purchasing program for outpatient hospitals and ambulatory surgical centers [3]	....	....	....	....	....	....	....	....	....	....	....	....	....
Expand basis for beneficiary assignment for Accountable Care Organizations	....	....	....	–10	–10	–10	–10	–10	–10	–10	–10	–30	–80
Reform physician self-referral law to better support and align with alternative payment models and to address overutilization [3]	....	....	....	....	....	....	....	....	....	....	....	....	....
Reprioritize primary and preventive care in Medicare	....	....	....	....	....	....	....	....	....	....	....	....	....
Require prior authorization when physicians order certain services excessively relative to their peers [3]	....	....	....	....	....	....	....	....	....	....	....	....	....
Reform and expand durable medical equipment competitive bidding	....	....	–390	–690	–740	–795	–855	–910	–985	–1,045	–1,110	–2,615	–7,520
Support coverage for innovative alternatives to durable medical equipment for treatment and management of diabetes [3]	....	....	....	....	....	....	....	....	....	....	....	....	....
Allow for Federal/State coordinated review of dual eligible Special Needs Plan marketing materials	....	....	....	....	....	....	....	....	....	....	....	....	....
Improve appeals notifications for dually eligible individuals in Integrated Health Plans	....	....	....	....	....	....	....	....	....	....	....	....	....
Clarify the Part D special enrollment period for dually eligible beneficiaries	....	–20	–20	–10	–20	–20	–20	–20	–20	–30	–30	–90	–210

Table S–6. Mandatory and Receipt Proposals—Continued

(Deficit increases (+) or decreases (–) in millions of dollars)

	2019	2020	2021	2022	2023	2024	2025	2026	2027	2028	2029	Totals 2020–2024	Totals 2020–2029
Give Medicare beneficiaries with high deductible health plans the option to make tax deductible contributions to Health Savings Accounts or Medical Savings Accounts [1]	....	....	601	1,066	1,287	1,492	1,597	1,682	1,764	1,825	1,283	4,446	12,597
Expand prior authorization to additional Medicare fee-for-service items at high risk of fraud, waste, and abuse	....	–430	–510	–540	–570	–610	–640	–680	–720	–760	–800	–2,660	–6,260
Prevent fraud by applying penalties on providers and suppliers who fail to update enrollment records	....	–2	–2	–3	–3	–3	–3	–4	–4	–4	–4	–13	–32
Require reporting on clearinghouses and billing agents when Medicare providers and suppliers enroll in the program	....	....	....	....	....	....	....	....	....	....	....	....	....
Ensure providers that violate Medicare's safety requirements and have harmed patients cannot quickly re-enter the program	....	....	....	....	....	....	....	....	....	....	....	....	....
Assess a penalty on physicians and practitioners who order services or supplies without proper documentation	....	....	....	....	....	....	....	....	....	....	....	....	....
Improve safety and quality of care by publicly reporting Medicare survey and certification reports conducted by accreditation organizations	....	....	....	....	....	....	....	....	....	....	....	....	....
Require providers and suppliers to produce Part B records to support Part D investigations or audits	....	....	....	....	....	....	....	....	....	....	....	....	....
Pass Treasury collection fees for CMS overpayment collections onto debtor	....	–20	–20	–20	–20	–20	–20	–20	–20	–20	–20	–100	–200
Improve efficiency and strengthen program integrity efforts in Medicare Parts C and D	....	....	....	....	....	....	....	....	....	....	....	....	....
Implement targeted risk-adjustment pre-payment review in Medicare Advantage	....	....	....	....	....	....	....	....	....	....	....	....	....
Clarify authority for the Healthcare Fraud Prevention Partnership	....	....	....	....	....	....	....	....	....	....	....	....	....
Extend flexibility in annual Open Payments reporting deadline	....	....	....	....	....	....	....	....	....	....	....	....	....
Require physician owned distributors to report in Open Payments	....	....	....	....	....	....	....	....	....	....	....	....	....
Create authority to revoke or deny Medicare billing privileges based on medical board or independent review organizations	....	....	....	....	....	....	....	....	....	....	....	....	....
Total, address wasteful spending, fraud, and abuse in Medicare	....	–9,492	–23,601	–30,747	–37,486	–43,986	–50,141	–55,752	–61,765	–68,754	–75,171	–145,312	–456,895

Table S–6. Mandatory and Receipt Proposals—Continued

(Deficit increases (+) or decreases (–) in millions of dollars)

	2019	2020	2021	2022	2023	2024	2025	2026	2027	2028	2029	Totals 2020–2024	Totals 2020–2029
Address wasteful spending, fraud, and abuse in Medicaid:													
Strengthen CMS's ability to recoup Medicaid improper payments	....	....	–100	–430	–460	–490	–520	–550	–590	–620	–660	–1,480	–4,420
Continue Medicaid Disproportionate Share Hospital (DSH) allotment reductions	....	....	....	....	....	....	....	–6,510	–6,490	–6,470	–6,450	....	–25,920
Clarify Medicaid treatment of third party payments for DSH allotments	....	....	....	....	....	....	....	....	....	....	....	....	....
Address inappropriate financing of Medicaid state share by public providers [3]	....	....	....	....	....	....	....	....	....	....	....	....	....
Prohibit Medicaid payments to public providers in excess of costs [3]	....	....	....	....	....	....	....	....	....	....	....	....	....
Consolidate provider screening for Medicaid and Children's Health Insurance Program (CHIP)	....	....	....	....	....	....	....	....	....	....	....	....	....
Provide flexibility for enrolling out-of-State providers in Medicaid	....	....	1	1	1	1	1	1	1	1	1	4	9
Streamline the Medicaid terminations process	....	....	....	....	....	....	....	....	....	....	....	....	....
Expand Medicaid Fraud Control Unit review to additional care settings [3]	....	....	....	....	....	....	....	....	....	....	....	....	....
Implement pre-payment controls to prevent inappropriate personal care services payments	....	–700	–730	–760	–800	–840	–880	–920	–970	–1,010	–1,060	–3,830	–8,670
Rescind remaining balances from the Medicaid Improvement Fund	....	....	–6	....	....	....	....	....	....	....	....	–6	–6
Total, address wasteful spending, fraud, and abuse in Medicaid	....	–700	–835	–1,189	–1,259	–1,329	–1,399	–7,979	–8,049	–8,099	–8,169	–5,312	–39,007
Other Medicaid reforms:													
Implement Medicaid community engagement requirement	....	–8,300	–10,900	–11,500	–12,100	–12,800	–13,500	–14,200	–14,900	–15,700	–16,500	–55,600	–130,400
Allow States to apply asset tests to Modified Adjusted Gross Income standard populations	....	–50	–100	–200	–210	–230	–240	–250	–260	–280	–290	–790	–2,110
Reduce maximum allowable home equity for Medicaid eligibility	....	....	–570	–610	–650	–690	–730	–780	–820	–870	–930	–2,520	–6,650
Require documentation of satisfactory immigration status before receipt of Medicaid benefits	....	–190	–190	–200	–210	–220	–230	–250	–260	–270	–290	–1,010	–2,310
Modify the Medicaid fair hearing requirement to eliminate duplicative appeals	....	....	....	....	....	....	....	....	....	....	....	....	....
Increase limit on Medicaid copayments for non-emergency use of emergency department	....	–60	–120	–120	–130	–140	–140	–150	–160	–170	–360	–570	–1,550

Table S–6. Mandatory and Receipt Proposals—Continued

(Deficit increases (+) or decreases (–) in millions of dollars)

	2019	2020	2021	2022	2023	2024	2025	2026	2027	2028	2029	Totals 2020–2024	Totals 2020–2029
Increase flexibility in the duration of section 1915(b) managed care waivers	....	....	....	....	....	....	....	....	....	....	....	....	....
Provide a pathway to make permanent established Medicaid managed care waivers	....	....	....	....	....	....	....	....	....	....	....	....	....
Total, other Medicaid reforms	....	–8,600	–11,880	–12,630	–13,300	–14,080	–14,840	–15,630	–16,400	–17,290	–18,370	–60,490	–143,020
CHIP:													
Strengthen the CHIP safety net for States	....	....	....	....	....	....	....	....	....	....	....	....	....
Public Health:													
Provide tax exemption for certain Health Resources and Services Administration (HRSA) and Indian Health Service (IHS) scholarship and loan repayment programs [1]	....	24	32	32	32	32	32	35	35	35	36	152	325
Align substance use disorder treatment privacy protections with other confidentiality protections	....	....	....	....	....	....	....	....	....	....	....	....	....
Extend Health Centers through 2021	....	1,800	3,920	2,160	80	40	....	....	....	....	....	8,000	8,000
Extend the National Health Service Corps through 2021	....	68	248	226	56	16	6	....	....	....	....	614	620
Extend Teaching Health Centers Graduate Medical Education through 2021	....	67	114	59	13	....	....	....	....	....	....	253	253
Extend the Special Diabetes Programs for the National Institutes of Health and the IHS through 2021	....	179	255	107	38	11	6	3	1	....	....	590	600
Extend Family to Family Health Information Centers through 2021	....	2	6	4	....	....	....	....	....	....	....	12	12
Extend Medicare enrollment assistance programs through 2021	....	38	38	....	....	....	....	....	....	....	....	76	76
Provide Federal Tort Claim Act coverage for IHS volunteers	....	....	....	....	....	....	....	....	....	....	....	....	....
Authorize IHS to establish concurrent Federal/State jurisdiction at IHS Federal enclave properties	....	....	....	....	....	....	....	....	....	....	....	....	....
Provide IHS discretionary use of all Title 38 personnel authorities	....	....	....	....	....	....	....	....	....	....	....	....	....
Meet IHS loan repayment and scholarship service obligations on a half-time basis	....	....	....	....	....	....	....	....	....	....	....	....	....
Reauthorize the Ryan White HIV/AIDS Program [3]	....	....	....	....	....	....	....	....	....	....	....	....	....
Total, public health	....	2,178	4,613	2,588	219	99	44	38	36	35	36	9,697	9,886
Other Health:													
Provide an appropriation to pay Cost-Sharing Reductions (CSR) [4]	–6,301	479	....	....	....	....	....	....	....	....	....	479	479

Table S–6. Mandatory and Receipt Proposals—Continued

(Deficit increases (+) or decreases (–) in millions of dollars)

	2019	2020	2021	2022	2023	2024	2025	2026	2027	2028	2029	Totals 2020–2024	Totals 2020–2029
Reduce the grace period for Exchange premiums [1]	....	–85	7	....	....	....	....	....	....	....	....	–78	–78
Introduce new minimum required contribution for premium tax credits [1]	....	–230	–115	....	....	....	....	....	....	....	....	–345	–345
Improve and expand access to Health Savings Accounts [1]	....	....	2,251	3,182	3,110	3,045	3,124	3,254	3,392	3,522	3,650	11,588	28,530
Reform medical liability [1]	....	–141	–478	–1,300	–2,111	–2,806	–3,887	–4,716	–5,061	–5,495	–5,516	–6,836	–31,511
Prohibit governmental discrimination against healthcare providers who refuse to cover abortion	....	....	....	....	....	....	....	....	....	....	....	....	....
Protect the religious liberty of child welfare providers	....	....	....	....	....	....	....	....	....	....	....	....	....
Provide CMS Program Management implementation funding	....	12	150	38	....	....	....	....	....	....	....	200	200
Modify the U.S. Public Health Service Commissioned Corps retirement pay funding source	....	....	....	....	....	....	....	....	....	....	....	....	....
Total, other health	–6,301	35	1,815	1,920	999	239	–763	–1,462	–1,669	–1,973	–1,866	5,008	–2,725
Interactions:													
Medicare interactions	....	223	456	574	648	713	761	807	861	912	969	2,614	6,924
Medicaid interactions	....	1,950	7,200	7,800	10,050	10,910	11,830	12,800	13,850	14,980	16,370	37,910	107,740
Total, interactions	....	2,173	7,656	8,374	10,698	11,623	12,591	13,607	14,711	15,892	17,339	40,524	114,664
Total, Health and Human Services (HHS)	–6,301	–13,972	–24,210	–35,032	–45,105	–54,307	–63,249	–75,712	–82,271	–90,354	–96,602	–172,626	–580,814
Homeland Security:													
Extend expiring Customs and Border Protection (CBP) fees	....	....	....	....	....	....	....	....	–967	–5,012	–5,109	....	–11,088
Increase customs user fees	....	–199	–177	–186	–196	–210	–222	–238	–249	–259	–265	–968	–2,201
Increase immigration user fees	....	–64	–9	–2	–10	–3	–19	–5	–21	–4	–13	–88	–150
Establish Electronic Visa Update System user fee [1]	....	....	....	....	....	....	....	....	....	....	....	....	....
Eliminate BrandUSA; make revenue available to CBP	....	–11	56	16	....	....	....	....	....	....	....	61	61
Make full Electronic System for Travel Authorization receipts available to CBP [1]	....	....	91	152	174	180	187	192	199	–4	–4	597	1,167
Establish an immigration services surcharge [1]	....	–466	–471	–479	–486	–494	–508	–523	–538	–554	–570	–2,396	–5,089
Increase worksite enforcement penalties [1]	....	–13	–14	–15	–15	–15	–15	–15	–15	–15	–15	–72	–147
Establish National Flood Insurance Program affordability assistance [5]	....	4	4	19	26	39	54	69	88	103	111	92	517
Transfer immigration examination fees	....	....	....	....	....	....	....	....	....	....	....	....	....
Reauthorize the Oil Spill Liability Trust Fund excise tax [1,6]	....	–403	–533	–539	–544	–551	–552	–536	–535	–543	–546	–2,570	–5,282
Total, Homeland Security	....	–1,152	–1,053	–1,034	–1,051	–1,054	–1,075	–1,056	–2,038	–6,288	–6,411	–5,344	–22,212

Table S–6. Mandatory and Receipt Proposals—Continued

(Deficit increases (+) or decreases (–) in millions of dollars)

	2019	2020	2021	2022	2023	2024	2025	2026	2027	2028	2029	Totals 2020–2024	Totals 2020–2029
Interior:													
Cancel Southern Nevada Public Land Management Act balances	....	–83	–69	–78	....	....	....	....	....	....	....	–230	–230
Repeal enhanced geothermal payments to counties	....	–4	–4	–4	–4	–4	–4	–4	–4	–4	–4	–20	–40
Reauthorize the Federal Lands Recreation Enhancement Act	....	....	....	....	....	....	....	....	....	....	....	....	....
Establish a Public Lands Infrastructure Fund	....	260	715	1,040	1,300	1,300	1,040	585	260	....	....	4,615	6,500
Total, Interior	....	173	642	958	1,296	1,296	1,036	581	256	–4	–4	4,365	6,230
Justice:													
Establish a definite annual funding level for the Crime Victims Fund	....	–3,426	–2,270	–1,779	–1,347	–200	–200	–200	–200	–200	–200	–9,022	–10,022
Labor:													
Improve Pension Benefit Guaranty Corporation (PBGC) Multiemployer solvency	....	65	–1,860	–1,925	–2,003	–2,005	781	–4,658	–2,086	–2,110	–2,117	–7,728	–17,918
Reform PBGC single-employer premiums	....	....	–233	–59	9	6	63	36	70	62	77	–277	31
Expand Foreign Labor Certification fees	....	....	....	....	....	....	....	....	....	....	....	....	....
Reform the Federal Employees' Compensation Act	....	–31	–26	–29	–18	–18	–19	–19	–20	–21	–19	–122	–220
Reform the Trade Adjustment Assistance program	....	–51	–125	–187	–172	–72	–7	–16	–45	–72	–102	–607	–849
Increase H–1B American Competitiveness and Workforce Improvement Act filing fee	....	–325	–207	–109	–19	....	....	....	....	....	....	–660	–660
Establish a paid parental leave program:													
Provide paid parental leave benefits [1,7]	....	750	750	1,310	1,958	2,161	2,357	2,543	2,718	2,879	3,027	6,929	20,453
Establish an Unemployment Insurance (UI) solvency standard [1]	....	....	....	–332	–678	–1,042	–1,472	–2,047	–404	–690	–1,062	–2,052	–7,727
Improve UI program integrity [1]	....	–103	–225	–258	–259	–258	–370	–190	–133	–193	–244	–1,103	–2,233
Total, establish a paid parental leave program	....	647	525	720	1,021	861	515	306	2,181	1,996	1,721	3,774	10,493
Total, Labor	....	305	–1,926	–1,589	–1,182	–1,228	1,333	–4,351	100	–145	–440	–5,620	–9,123
Transportation:													
Eliminate Off-System Bridges Set-Aside	....	....	....	....	....	....	....	....	....	....	....	....	....
Treasury:													
Provide authority for Bureau of Engraving and Printing to construct a new facility [1]	–42	–5	–3	83	–360	–54	19	–3	–223	–3	....	–339	–549
Increase and extend guarantee fee charged by Government Sponsored Enterprises	....	–224	–1,014	–1,616	–3,003	–4,352	–5,108	–4,971	–4,371	–3,771	–3,284	–10,209	–31,714

Table S–6. Mandatory and Receipt Proposals—Continued

(Deficit increases (+) or decreases (–) in millions of dollars)

	2019	2020	2021	2022	2023	2024	2025	2026	2027	2028	2029	Totals 2020–2024	Totals 2020–2029
Subject Financial Research Fund to appropriations [1,6]	....	....	34	–12	–17	–17	–17	–17	–17	–17	–17	–12	–97
Increase collections of delinquent Federal non-tax debt	....	–32	–32	–32	–32	–32	–32	–32	–32	–32	–32	–160	–320
Increase and streamline recovery of unclaimed assets	....	–6	–6	–6	–6	–6	–6	–6	–6	–6	–6	–30	–60
Implement tax enforcement program integrity cap adjustment [1]	....	–160	–818	–1,895	–3,166	–4,558	–5,899	–6,880	–7,510	–7,942	–8,241	–10,597	–47,069
Increase discretionary outlays from tax enforcement program integrity cap adjustment (non-add)	....	*320*	*693*	*1,040*	*1,386*	*1,737*	*1,850*	*1,865*	*1,875*	*1,885*	*1,893*	*5,176*	*14,544*
Increase oversight of paid tax return preparers [1]	....	–25	–35	–39	–44	–48	–53	–57	–62	–69	–75	–191	–507
Provide more flexible authority for the Internal Revenue Service to address correctable errors [1]	....	–1,061	–1,584	–1,632	–1,685	–1,750	–1,809	–1,871	–1,934	–2,014	–2,086	–7,712	–17,426
Repeal the qualified plug-in electric drive motor vehicle credit [1]	....	–34	–379	–386	–381	–319	–234	–207	–221	–208	–156	–1,499	–2,525
Repeal exclusion of utility conservation subsidies [1]	....	–2	–10	–9	–8	–8	–7	–7	–6	–6	–5	–37	–68
Repeal accelerated depreciation for renewable energy property [1]	....	–127	–395	–591	–655	–688	–690	–622	–534	–448	–352	–2,456	–5,102
Repeal energy investment credit [1]	....	160	–274	–1,184	–1,457	–1,382	–1,254	–1,105	–1,019	–957	–916	–4,137	–9,388
Repeal credit for residential energy efficient property [1]	....	–374	–676	–192	–34	....	....	....	....	....	....	–1,276	–1,276
Total, Treasury	–42	–1,890	–5,192	–7,511	–10,848	–13,214	–15,090	–15,778	–15,935	–15,473	–15,170	–38,655	–116,101
Veterans Affairs (VA):													
Cap Post–9/11 GI Bill flight training programs at public schools	....	–28	–29	–30	–31	–32	–33	–34	–35	–38	–39	–150	–329
Enhance burial benefits for veterans	....	3	3	3	8	3	4	4	13	2	5	20	48
Reinstate Cost-of-Living Adjustment round-down	....	–36	–84	–129	–173	–229	–255	–266	–282	–297	–314	–651	–2,065
Standardize and enhance VA Compensation and Pension benefit programs	....	–234	–269	–278	–288	–298	–309	–320	–331	–103	–269	–1,367	–2,699
Standardize and improve veteran vocational rehabilitation and education benefit programs	....	2	1	1	1	1	1	1	1	1	2	6	12
Standardize and improve Specially Adapted Housing programs	....	....	1	1	1	1	....	....	....	....	....	4	4
Total, Veterans Affairs	....	–293	–377	–432	–482	–554	–592	–615	–634	–435	–615	–2,138	–5,029
Corps of Engineers:													
Divest Washington Aqueduct	....	....	....	–123	....	....	....	....	....	....	....	–123	–123
Reform inland waterways financing [1]	....	–178	–178	–178	–178	–178	–178	–178	–178	–178	–178	–890	–1,780
Total, Corps of Engineers	....	–178	–178	–301	–178	–178	–178	–178	–178	–178	–178	–1,013	–1,903

Table S–6. Mandatory and Receipt Proposals—Continued

(Deficit increases (+) or decreases (–) in millions of dollars)

	2019	2020	2021	2022	2023	2024	2025	2026	2027	2028	2029	Totals 2020–2024	Totals 2020–2029
Environmental Protection Agency:													
Expand use of pesticide licensing fees	....	5	4	4	4	4	3	2	1	1	1	21	29
General Services Administration (GSA) [8]:													
Increase employee contributions to 50 percent of cost, phased in at one percent per year [1]	....	....	–2,121	–4,400	–6,687	–8,627	–10,191	–11,505	–11,699	–11,762	–11,819	–21,835	–78,811
Implement defined contribution system for term employees [1]	....	33	90	92	93	95	98	100	102	104	106	403	913
Eliminate Federal Employees Retirement System COLA, reduce Civil Service Retirement System COLA by 0.5 percent	....	–1,308	–2,074	–2,910	–3,815	–4,789	–5,832	–6,949	–8,140	–9,409	–10,757	–14,896	–55,983
Eliminate the Special Retirement Supplement	....	–194	–601	–1,045	–1,529	–1,900	–2,141	–2,391	–2,650	–2,918	–3,196	–5,269	–18,565
Change retirement calculation from high–three years to high–five years	....	–359	–429	–502	–575	–650	–729	–810	–894	–980	–1,068	–2,515	–6,996
Reduce the G Fund interest rate	....	–3,549	–2,157	–2,263	–784	–806	–1,032	–1,305	–1,415	–1,536	–1,627	–9,559	–16,474
Loss of mandatory offsetting receipts from GSA proposals	....	....	8,630	10,742	13,050	15,037	16,662	18,219	18,655	18,958	19,253	47,459	139,206
Discretionary effect of GSA proposals	....	....	–6,441	–7,668	–8,908	–9,816	–10,400	–10,873	–10,646	–10,346	–10,046	–32,833	–85,144
Postal effect of GSA proposals	....	....	1,646	1,989	2,212	2,412	2,590	2,595	2,602	2,608	2,617	8,259	21,271
Federal Employees Health Benefits (FEHB) Program:													
Modify the Government contribution to FEHB premiums	....	....	....	–134	–209	–222	–235	–249	–263	–278	–294	–565	–1,884
Provide tax preemption for Federal Employees Dental/Vision Program	....	....	....	....	....	....	....	....	....	....	....	....	....
Total, Federal Employees Health Benefits (FEHB) Program	....	....	....	–134	–209	–222	–235	–249	–263	–278	–294	–565	–1,884
Total, General Services Administration	....	–5,377	–3,457	–6,099	–7,152	–9,266	–11,210	–13,168	–14,348	–15,559	–16,831	–31,351	–102,467
Other Independent Agencies:													
Restructure the Consumer Financial Protection Bureau	....	–23	–508	–515	–527	–539	–552	–566	–579	–593	–607	–2,112	–5,009
Eliminate the Securities and Exchange Commission Reserve Fund	....	....	–17	–41	–50	–50	–50	–50	–50	–50	–50	–158	–408
Allow D.C. Courts to retain bar exam and application fees [9]	....	....	....	....	....	....	....	....	....	....	....	....	....
Mandatory effects of agency eliminations	....	....	....	....	....	....	....	....	....	....	....	....	....
Federal Communications Commission:													
Enact Spectrum License User Fee	....	–50	–150	–300	–450	–500	–500	–500	–500	–500	–500	–1,450	–3,950
Conduct spectrum auctions below six gigahertz	....	–300	–300	....	....	....	....	....	....	....	–6,000	–600	–6,600
Total, Federal Communications Commission	....	–350	–450	–300	–450	–500	–500	–500	–500	–500	–6,500	–2,050	–10,550

Table S–6. Mandatory and Receipt Proposals—Continued

(Deficit increases (+) or decreases (–) in millions of dollars)

	2019	2020	2021	2022	2023	2024	2025	2026	2027	2028	2029	Totals 2020–2024	Totals 2020–2029
Postal Service:													
Reform the Postal Service	....	–4,157	–7,837	–8,384	–9,023	–9,698	–10,388	–11,153	–11,991	–12,802	–12,794	–39,099	–98,227
Tennessee Valley Authority:													
Divest Tennessee Valley Authority transmission assets	....	229	–4,743	–124	–124	–124	–124	–124	–124	–124	–124	–4,886	–5,506
Total, other independent agencies	....	–4,301	–13,555	–9,364	–10,174	–10,911	–11,614	–12,393	–13,244	–14,069	–20,075	–48,305	–119,700
Cross-cutting reforms:													
Authorize additional Afghan Special Immigrant Visas	....	25	37	39	36	33	32	29	28	27	27	170	313
Eliminate allocations to the Housing Trust Fund and Capital Magnet Fund [1]	....	–128	–145	–220	–293	–348	–367	–379	–398	–401	–404	–1,134	–3,083
Extend Joint Committee mandatory sequestration	....	....	....	....	....	....	....	....	10,016	–25,932	–34,280	....	–50,196
Improve clarity in worker classification and information reporting requirements [1]	....	–86	–104	–138	–177	–206	–235	–271	–298	–315	–337	–711	–2,167
Empowering States and consumers to reform healthcare [1]:													
Proposal modeled after the Graham-Cassidy-Heller-Johnson bill:													
Medicaid reforms	....	1,280	–69,795	–101,306	–103,061	–113,976	–126,207	–130,542	–145,462	–160,828	–178,178	–386,858	–1,128,075
Market-based healthcare grant programs	....	....	146,000	157,000	168,000	179,000	190,000	190,000	210,000	220,000	230,000	650,000	1,690,000
Other	....	12,149	–19,030	–43,649	–50,008	–50,372	–53,071	–56,041	–59,468	–62,126	–65,068	–150,910	–446,684
Total, proposal modeled after the Graham-Cassidy-Heller-Johnson bill	....	13,429	57,175	12,045	14,931	14,652	10,722	3,417	5,070	–2,954	–13,246	112,232	115,241
Additional deficit reduction:													
Medicaid reforms	....	....	–100	–3,100	–15,860	–23,140	–29,130	–36,510	–42,500	–49,900	–57,200	–42,200	–257,440
Market-based healthcare grant programs	....	....	–23,240	–31,417	–39,529	–47,574	–55,551	–52,459	–69,296	–76,060	–82,749	–141,760	–477,875
State implementation	....	1,000	750	250	....	....	....	....	....	....	....	2,000	2,000
Other	....	–10,000	–21,000	–5,000	....	–750	–750	–750	–750	–750	–750	–36,750	–40,500
Total, additional deficit reduction	....	–9,000	–43,590	–39,267	–55,389	–71,464	–85,431	–89,719	–112,546	–126,710	–140,699	–218,710	–773,815
Total, empowering States and consumers to reform healthcare	....	4,429	13,585	–27,222	–40,458	–56,812	–74,709	–86,302	–107,476	–129,664	–153,945	–106,478	–658,574
Reform welfare programs:													
Reform the Supplemental Nutrition Assistance Program	....	–17,401	–19,734	–21,348	–21,934	–22,533	–23,095	–23,659	–23,504	–23,364	–23,209	–102,950	–219,781
Reduce TANF block grant	....	–1,099	–1,447	–1,519	–1,552	–1,613	–1,609	–1,601	–1,620	–1,624	–1,600	–7,230	–15,284
Strengthen TANF	....	....	....	....	....	....	....	....	....	....	....	....	....
Eliminate the TANF Contingency Fund	....	–545	–608	–608	–608	–608	–608	–608	–608	–608	–608	–2,977	–6,017
Get noncustodial parents to work	....	4	5	7	8	9	10	11	13	14	15	33	96

Table S–6. Mandatory and Receipt Proposals—Continued

(Deficit increases (+) or decreases (–) in millions of dollars)

	2019	2020	2021	2022	2023	2024	2025	2026	2027	2028	2029	Totals 2020–2024	Totals 2020–2029
Strengthen Child Support enforcement and establishment	....	–24	–40	–58	–66	–76	–77	–79	–81	–84	–86	–264	–671
Establish a Child Support technology fund	....	35	–42	–52	–63	–74	–150	–163	–177	–242	–257	–196	–1,185
Eliminate SSBG	....	–1,360	–1,632	–1,700	–1,700	–1,700	–1,700	–1,700	–1,700	–1,700	–1,700	–8,092	–16,592
Shift SSBG expenditures to Foster Care and Permanency	....	17	21	22	22	22	22	22	22	22	22	104	214
Require Social Security Number for Child Tax Credit, Earned Income Tax Credit, and credit for other dependents [1]	....	–1,780	–6,664	–6,754	–6,957	–7,104	–7,269	–7,531	–7,702	–7,902	–8,237	–29,259	–67,900
Promote Opportunity and Economic Mobility Demonstrations	....	22	41	60	79	98	78	59	40	21	2	300	500
Total, reform welfare programs	....	–22,131	–30,100	–31,950	–32,771	–33,579	–34,398	–35,249	–35,317	–35,467	–35,658	–150,531	–326,620
Reform Federal disability programs and improve payment integrity:													
Improve Supplemental Security Income (SSI) youth transition to work	....	–5	–26	–8	–39	–158	–292	–432	–580	–742	–839	–236	–3,121
Test new approaches to increase labor force participation	....	100	100	100	100	100	–2,480	–5,073	–9,094	–13,636	–17,769	500	–47,552
Reduce 12 month retroactive Disability Insurance (DI) benefits to six months	....	–316	–568	–741	–940	–1,044	–1,133	–1,214	–1,285	–1,352	–1,409	–3,609	–10,002
Create a family maximum benefit structure for SSI disabled children in multirecipient families	....	–784	–800	–865	–821	–782	–867	–888	–907	–997	–885	–4,052	–8,596
Offset overlapping unemployment and disability payments [1]	....	....	–76	–200	–241	–264	–272	–293	–306	–315	–321	–781	–2,288
Eliminate Workers Compensation reverse offsets	....	....	....	–21	–22	–23	–25	–26	–28	–30	–32	–66	–207
Change the representative fee and approval process	....	....	3	15	25	28	21	24	22	21	22	71	181
Simplify Administration of the SSI Program	....	....	–382	–98	–69	–46	–34	–23	–11	2	13	–595	–648
Allow State hearing officers to hold disability hearings	....	....	....	....	....	....	....	....	....	....	....	....	....
Eliminate travel reimbursement for claimants' representatives	....	....	....	....	....	....	....	....	....	....	....	....	....
Modernize the commissioner's collection of evidence to determine entitlement or eligibility	....	....	....	....	....	....	....	....	....	....	....	....	....
Provide additional debt collection authority for civil monetary penalties and assessments	....	....	....	....	....	....	....	....	....	....	....	....	....
Allow Government-wide use of CBP entry/exit data to prevent improper payments	....	....	....	–1	–5	–11	–18	–27	–35	–43	–41	–17	–181

Table S–6. Mandatory and Receipt Proposals—Continued

(Deficit increases (+) or decreases (–) in millions of dollars)

	2019	2020	2021	2022	2023	2024	2025	2026	2027	2028	2029	Totals 2020–2024	Totals 2020–2029
Authorize Social Security Administration to use all collection tools to recover funds in certain scenarios	....	....	–2	–3	–4	–5	–5	–6	–6	–7	–8	–14	–46
Hold fraud facilitators liable for overpayments	....	....	....	–1	–2	–2	–1	–1	–1	....	–2	–5	–10
Expand mandatory electronic filing of W–2s [1]	....	–39	–37	–36	–33	–32	–31	–30	–28	–27	–26	–177	–319
Increase overpayment collection threshold for Old Age, Survivors, and Disability Insurance	....	–12	–77	–100	–110	–135	–161	–181	–237	–254	–251	–434	–1,518
Use death master file to prevent improper payments	....	....	....	....	....	....	....	....	....	....	....	....	....
Exclude SSA debts from discharge in bankruptcy	....	–4	–12	–20	–24	–29	–32	–34	–37	–39	–43	–89	–274
Improve collection of pension information from States and localities	....	18	28	24	–474	–1,135	–1,614	–1,735	–1,645	–1,547	–1,429	–1,539	–9,509
Total, reform Federal disability programs and improve payment integrity	....	–1,042	–1,849	–1,955	–2,659	–3,538	–6,944	–9,939	–14,178	–18,966	–23,020	–11,043	–84,090
Implement an infrastructure initiative:													
Support major investment in infrastructure	....	4,750	23,750	38,000	47,500	38,000	19,000	9,500	4,750	4,750	....	152,000	190,000
Establish a Federal Capital Revolving Fund [10]	....	269	2,046	2,167	2,001	1,834	267	201	134	67	1	8,317	8,987
Total, implement an infrastructure initiative	....	5,019	25,796	40,167	49,501	39,834	19,267	9,701	4,884	4,817	1	160,317	198,987
Total, cross-cutting reforms	....	–13,914	7,220	–21,279	–26,821	–54,616	–97,354	–122,410	–142,739	–205,901	–247,616	–109,410	–925,430
Total, mandatory and receipt proposals	**–6,343**	**–51,750**	**–60,368**	**–100,649**	**–125,184**	**–169,001**	**–225,591**	**–273,482**	**–301,407**	**–379,318**	**–436,065**	**–506,952**	**–2,122,815**

Note: For receipt effects, positive figures indicate lower receipts. For outlay effects, positive figures indicate higher outlays. For net costs, positive figures indicate higher deficits.

[1] The estimates for this proposal include effects on receipts. The receipt effects included in the totals above are as follows:

	2019	2020	2021	2022	2023	2024	2025	2026	2027	2028	2029	2020–2024	2020–2029
Establish Education Freedom Scholarships	....	893	4,847	4,928	5,006	4,974	5,036	4,916	4,934	4,960	4,994	20,648	45,488
Give Medicare beneficiaries with high deductible health plans the option to make tax deductible contributions to Health Savings Accounts or Medical Savings Accounts	....	....	601	1,056	1,267	1,472	1,577	1,652	1,724	1,785	1,223	4,396	12,357
Provide tax exemption for certain HRSA and IHS scholarship and loan repayment programs	....	24	32	32	32	32	32	35	35	35	36	152	325
Reduce the grace period for Exchange premiums	....	–47	20	....	....	....	....	....	....	....	....	–27	–27
Introduce new minimum required contribution for premium tax credits	....	....	–38	....	....	....	....	....	....	....	....	–38	–38

Table S–6. Mandatory and Receipt Proposals—Continued

(Deficit increases (+) or decreases (–) in millions of dollars)

	2019	2020	2021	2022	2023	2024	2025	2026	2027	2028	2029	Totals 2020–2024	Totals 2020–2029
Improve and expand access to Health Savings Accounts	....	....	2,122	2,997	2,933	2,872	2,948	3,077	3,216	3,339	3,467	10,924	26,971
Reform medical liability	....	–18	–64	–94	–117	–134	–183	–147	–33	....	....	–427	–790
Establish Electronic Visa Update System user fee	....	–34	–38	–42	–47	–52	–58	–64	–72	–79	–88	–213	–574
Make full Electronic System for Travel Authorization (ESTA) receipts available to CBP	....	....	....	....	....	....	1	....	....	–209	–216	....	–424
Establish an immigration services surcharge	....	–466	–471	–479	–486	–494	–508	–523	–538	–554	–570	–2,396	–5,089
Increase worksite enforcement penalties	....	–13	–14	–15	–15	–15	–15	–15	–15	–15	–15	–72	–147
Reauthorize the Oil Spill Liability Trust Fund excise tax	....	–403	–533	–539	–544	–551	–552	–536	–535	–543	–546	–2,570	–5,282
Provide paid parental leave benefits	....	....	....	–538	–803	–887	–966	–1,042	–1,113	–1,180	–1,241	–2,228	–7,770
Establish an Unemployment Insurance (UI) solvency standard	....	....	....	–332	–678	–1,042	–1,472	–2,047	–404	–690	–1,062	–2,052	–7,727
Improve UI program integrity	....	....	1	8	22	39	–54	143	214	169	140	70	682
Provide authority for Bureau of Engraving and Printing to construct new facility	–42	–5	–3	83	–360	–54	19	–3	–223	–3	....	–339	–549
Subject Financial Reasearch Fund to appropriations	....	....	51	51	51	51	51	51	51	51	51	204	459
Implement tax enforcement program integrity cap adjustment	....	–160	–818	–1,895	–3,166	–4,558	–5,899	–6,880	–7,510	–7,942	–8,241	–10,597	–47,069
Increase oversight of paid tax return preparers	....	–19	–19	–21	–24	–26	–29	–32	–35	–39	–43	–109	–287
Provide more flexible authority for the Internal Revenue Service to address correctable errors	....	–419	–634	–666	–700	–736	–773	–812	–852	–893	–937	–3,155	–7,422
Repeal the qualified plug-in electric drive motor vehicle credit	....	–34	–379	–386	–381	–319	–234	–207	–221	–208	–156	–1,499	–2,525
Repeal exclusion of utility conservation subsidies	....	–2	–10	–9	–8	–8	–7	–7	–6	–6	–5	–37	–68
Repeal accelerated depreciation for renewable energy property	....	–127	–395	–591	–655	–688	–690	–622	–534	–448	–352	–2,456	–5,102
Repeal energy investment credit	....	160	–274	–1,184	–1,457	–1,382	–1,254	–1,105	–1,019	–957	–916	–4,137	–9,388
Repeal credit for residential energy efficient property	....	–374	–676	–192	–34	....	....	....	....	....	....	–1,276	–1,276
Reform inland waterways financing	....	–178	–178	–178	–178	–178	–178	–178	–178	–178	–178	–890	–1,780
Increase employee contributions to 50 percent of cost, phased in at 1 percent per year	....	....	–2,121	–4,400	–6,687	–8,627	–10,191	–11,505	–11,699	–11,762	–11,819	–21,835	–78,811
Implement defined contribution system for term employees	....	33	90	92	93	95	98	100	102	104	106	403	913
Expand mandatory electronic filing of W–2s	....	–12	–12	–12	–11	–11	–11	–11	–10	–10	–10	–58	–110
Eliminate allocations to the Housing Trust Fund and Capital Magnet Fund	....	–64	–72	–65	–66	–66	–66	–66	–67	–68	–70	–333	–670

Table S–6. Mandatory and Receipt Proposals—Continued

(Deficit increases (+) or decreases (–) in millions of dollars)

	2019	2020	2021	2022	2023	2024	2025	2026	2027	2028	2029	Totals 2020–2024	Totals 2020–2029
Improve clarity in worker classification and information reporting requirements	....	–86	–124	–147	–188	–220	–249	–282	–302	–321	–341	–765	–2,260
Empowering States and consumers to reform healthcare	....	959	–24	3,489	4,014	4,355	4,081	3,688	3,415	3,737	3,901	12,793	31,615
Require Social Security Number for Child Tax Credit, Earned Income Tax Credit, and credit for other dependents	....	–1,780	–3,587	–3,662	–3,764	–3,887	–4,028	–4,175	–4,328	–4,501	–4,694	–16,680	–38,406
Offset overlapping unemployment and disability payments	....	....	....	....	1	7	18	15	17	20	28	8	106
Total receipt effects of mandatory proposals	–42	–2,172	–2,720	–2,711	–6,950	–10,038	–13,556	–16,582	–15,986	–16,406	–17,554	–24,591	–104,675

[2] The single income-driven repayment plan proposal has sizable interactive effects with the proposals to eliminate subsidized loans and Public Service Loan Forgiveness. These effects, $19.7 billion over 10 years, are included in the single income-driven repayment plan subtotal.

[3] Estimates were not available at the time of Budget publication.

[4] Fully fund CSR payments for qualified health plans that did not increase premiums to account for non-payment of CSRs.

[5] While this proposal increases outlays to provide means-tested assistance to low-income policyholders, the National Flood Insurance Program is also accelerating premium increases on other policyholders that currently do not pay full-risk premiums.

[6] Net of income offsets.

[7] The paid parental leave proposal consists of $28,233 million in benefit and program administration costs, offset by $7,770 million in savings associated with increased State revenues.

[8] The President's Budget proposes to transfer functions of the Office of Personnel Management to the GSA. For additional information on this reorganization proposal, please consult the Reorganization Chapter of the *Analytical Perspectives* volume.

[9] The proposal would allow the D.C. Courts to retain a portion of the bar examination and application fees it currently deposits into the D.C. Crime Victim's Compensation Fund. Retained fees are estimated at $360,000 annually beginning in 2019.

[10] The Federal Capital Revolving Fund is capitalized with $10 billion in mandatory funds in 2020. Agency repayments to the fund are reflected as offsetting collections, which reduce the total outlays estimated from the fund over the 10-year window. However, the initial $10 billion in capitalization funding is fully expended by 2024.

Table S–7. Proposed Discretionary Funding Levels in 2020 Budget

(Net budget authority in billions of dollars)

	2019	2020	2021	2022	2023	2024	2025	2026	2027	2028	2029	Totals 2020–2029
Defense:												
Current Law Funding Levels[1]	647	576	590	605	620	635	651	667	684	701	719	6,448
Proposed Base Changes[2]	....	....	....	*+135*	*+138*	*+139*	*+91*	*+91*	*+90*	*+89*	*+88*	*+861*
Defense Cap Adjustments:[3]												
Emergency Requirements	....	*9*	....	....	....	....	....	....	....	....	....	*9*
Overseas Contingency Operations (OCO) levels	*69*	*165*	*156*	*20*	*20*	*10*	*10*	*10*	*10*	*10*	*10*	*420*
Total, Defense	**716**	**750**	**746**	**760**	**778**	**784**	**752**	**768**	**784**	**800**	**817**	**7,739**
Non-Defense:												
Current Law Funding Levels[1]	597	543	556	570	584	599	613	629	645	661	677	6,076
Proposed Base Changes[2]	....	....	*–24*	*–49*	*–73*	*–98*	*–122*	*–148*	*–174*	*–199*	*–224*	*–1,110*
Proposed Base Funding	**597**	**543**	**532**	**521**	**511**	**501**	**491**	**481**	**471**	**462**	**453**	**4,966**
Federal Employee Retirement Cost Share Reduction Proposal:[4]	....	....	*–6*	*–8*	*–9*	*–10*	*–10*	*–11*	*–11*	*–10*	*–10*	*–85*
Non-Defense Cap Adjustments:												
OCO[5]	12	....	....	....	....	....	....	....	....	....	....	....
Emergency Requirements	2	....	....	....	....	....	....	....	....	....	....	....
Program Integrity	2	2	3	3	4	4	5	5	5	5	5	40
Disaster Relief[6]	7	19	7	7	7	7	7	7	7	7	7	86
Wildfire Suppression	....	2	2	2	2	2	2	2	2	2	2	23
Total, Non-Defense Cap Adjustments	**23**	**24**	**12**	**13**	**13**	**14**	**14**	**14**	**14**	**15**	**15**	**148**
Total, Non-Defense with all Adjustments	**620**	**567**	**538**	**526**	**515**	**505**	**495**	**484**	**475**	**466**	**458**	**5,029**
Total, Discretionary Budget Authority	**1,336**	**1,317**	**1,284**	**1,286**	**1,293**	**1,289**	**1,247**	**1,252**	**1,259**	**1,266**	**1,275**	**12,768**
Memorandum - Appropriations Counted Outside of Discretionary Caps:												
21st Century Cures Appropriations[7]	*1*	*1*	*	*1*	*1*	*	*	*	....	....	....	*4*
Non-BBEDCA Emergency Funding[8]	....	*–5*	....	....	....	....	....	....	....	....	....	*–5*

* $500 million or less.

[1] The current law funding levels presented here are equal to the caps estimated for 2019 through 2021 in the Balanced Budget and Emergency Deficit Control Act of 1985 (BBEDCA) with separate categories of funding for "defense" (or Function 050) and "non-defense" (NDD) programs and include Office of Management and Budget (OMB) estimates of Joint Committee enforcement (also known as "sequestration"). For 2022 through 2029, programs are assumed to grow at current services growth rates.

[2] The 2020 Budget proposes funding levels at the existing 2020 BBEDCA caps for defense and NDD programs. In 2021, the Administration proposes no change to the existing defense and NDD caps but would fund defense programs at the existing cap while beginning an annual two percent (or "2-penny") decrease to NDD programs. After 2021, the 2020 Budget proposes defense caps through 2029 that resource national defense requirements while NDD caps are proposed that would continue the 2-penny decrease for each year.

Table S–7. Proposed Discretionary Funding Levels in 2020 Budget—Continued

(Net budget authority in billions of dollars)

[3] The 2020 Budget proposes to hold the national defense base budget to the current law BBEDCA cap levels for national defense programs in 2020 and 2021. In order to fully resource national defense requirements, funding above the current law caps will also be necessary. The Budget therefore increases OCO amounts in 2020 and 2021 to nearly $165 billion and $156 billion, respectively. These amounts fund direct war costs, enduring in-theater support, and certain base budget requirements. In addition, more than $9 billion is requested in 2020 as an emergency requirement to address border security and hurricane recovery. After 2021, which is the final year of the discretionary caps in current law, outyear OCO amounts for 2022 and 2023 would be $20 billion in each year and $10 billion in 2024, consistent with the outyear OCO amounts included in OMB's 2019 Mid-Session Review. 2025 through 2029 amounts reflect a notional $10 billion placeholder for OCO consistent with a potential transition of certain OCO costs into the base budget while continuing to fund contingency operations. The placeholder amounts for 2025 through 2029 do not reflect specific decisions or assumptions about OCO funding in any particular year.

[4] This adjustment reflects savings from a reform proposed in the 2020 Budget that would reduce Federal agency costs through changes to current civilian employee retirement plans. After 2021, the Administration supports reductions to its proposed NDD caps for this reform.

[5] The 2020 Budget continues the Administration's policy to shift NDD OCO amounts into base discretionary funding. No NDD OCO amounts are proposed in 2020 or the outyears.

[6] "Disaster Relief" appropriations are amounts designated as such by the Congress provided they are for activities carried out pursuant to a Presidential disaster declaration under the Robert T. Stafford Disaster Relief and Emergency Assistance Act. These amounts are held to a funding ceiling that is determined annually according to a statutory formula. Based on its 2020 Budget assumptions, OMB estimates the 2020 ceiling to be more than $21 billion and the Administration is requesting more than $19 billion for Disaster Relief in 2020 to address significant and unprecedented recovery needs of recent hurricanes and wildfires. The Budget does not explicitly request disaster-designated appropriations in any year after 2020 and a placeholder set at the 10-year average level is included in each of the outyears. The Administration's disaster relief request is discussed in greater detail in the Budget Process chapter of the *Analytical Perspectives* volume of the Budget.

[7] The 21st Century Cures Act permitted funds to be appropriated each year and not counted towards the discretionary caps so long as the appropriations were specifically provided for the authorized purposes. These amounts are displayed outside of the discretionary totals for this reason and the levels included through the budget window reflect authorized levels.

[8] The 2020 Budget includes permanent cancellations of balances of emergency funding in the Departments of Energy and Housing and Urban Development that were not designated pursuant to BBEDCA. These cancellations are not being re-designated as emergency, therefore no savings are being achieved under the caps nor will the caps be adjusted for these cancellations.

Table S–8. 2020 Discretionary Overview by Major Agency

(Net budget authority in billions of dollars)

	2019 Estimate[1]	2020 Request	2020 Request less 2019 Estimate	
			Dollar	Percent
Base, OCO, and Program Integrity Discretionary Funding:				
Cabinet Departments:				
Agriculture[2]	24.4	20.8	–3.6	–14.8%
Commerce[1]	12.3	12.3	+*	+0.4%
Defense[3]	685.0	718.3	+33.4	+4.9%
Education	70.5	62.0	–8.5	–12.0%
Education, excluding Pell Grant cancellations	*71.1*	*64.0*	*–7.1*	*–10.0%*
Pell Grant cancellations	*–0.6*	*–2.0*	*–1.4*	*N/A*
Energy	35.5	31.7	–3.8	–10.8%
National Nuclear Security Administration	*15.1*	*16.5*	*+1.3*	*+8.9%*
Other Energy	*20.4*	*15.2*	*–5.2*	*–25.4%*
Health and Human Services:[4,5]	101.7	89.6	–12.1	–11.9%
Homeland Security (DHS)	48.1	51.7	+3.6	+7.4%
Housing and Urban Development (HUD):				
HUD gross total (excluding receipts)	*52.7*	*44.1*	*–8.6*	*–16.4%*
HUD receipts	*–9.3*	*–6.5*	*+2.8*	*–30.0%*
Interior	14.0	12.5	–1.5	–10.9%
Justice	29.9	29.2	–0.7	–2.3%
Labor	12.1	10.9	–1.2	–9.7%
State and Other International Programs[2,6]	55.8	42.8	–13.0	–23.3%
Transportation	27.3	21.4	–5.9	–21.5%
Treasury[7]	12.9	13.1	+0.2	+1.5%
Veterans Affairs	86.6	93.1	+6.5	+7.5%
Major Agencies:				
Corps of Engineers	7.0	4.8	–2.2	–31.0%
Environmental Protection Agency	8.8	6.1	–2.8	–31.2%
National Aeronautics and Space Administration	20.7	21.0	+0.3	+1.4%
National Science Foundation	7.8	7.1	–0.7	–9.0%
Small Business Administration	0.7	0.7	–*	–5.1%
Social Security Administration[4]	10.5	10.1	–0.4	–3.5%
Other Agencies	21.3	19.1	–2.1	–10.0%
Changes in mandatory programs	–7.7	–20.0	–12.2	N/A
Adjustment for 2019 Assumptions[2]	–0.9	....	+0.9	N/A
Subtotal, Base, OCO, and Program Integrity Funding	**1,327.7**	**1,296.0**	**–31.7**	**–2.4%**
Other Non-Defense Funding, including Cap Adjustments:				
Emergency Requirements:				
HUD	1.7	....	–1.7	N/A
Disaster Relief:[8]				
DHS	7.4	19.4	+12.1	+163.7%

Table S–8. 2020 Discretionary Overview by Major Agency—Continued

(Net budget authority in billions of dollars)

	2019 Estimate[1]	2020 Request	2020 Request less 2019 Estimate: Dollar	2020 Request less 2019 Estimate: Percent
Wildfire Suppression:				
Agriculture	....	2.0	+2.0	N/A
Interior	....	0.3	+0.3	N/A
Subtotal, Wildfire Suppression	....	2.3	+2.3	N/A
Non-BBEDCA Emergency Appropriations:				
Energy and HUD[9]	....	–4.9	–4.9	N/A
Subtotal, Other Non-Defense Funding	**9.0**	**16.8**	**+7.8**	**+85.8%**
Total, Discretionary Budget Authority	**1,336.7**	**1,312.8**	**–24.0**	**–1.8%**
Defense Total	*716.0*	*750.0*	*+34.0*	*+4.7%*
Non-Defense Total	*620.7*	*562.8*	*–58.0*	*–9.3%*
Memorandum, Non-Defense "Program Level" Budget Authority:				
2020 Non-Defense "Program Level" Compared to 2019 Cap	*597.0*	*569.4*	*–27.6*	*–4.6%*
Significant Non-Defense Offsets:				
Proposed cancellations		*–6.4*		
HHS changes in mandatory programs		*–19.7*		
Non-Defense Discretionary Budget Authority at 2020 cap		*543.2*		

* $50 million or less.

[1] At the time the 2020 Budget was prepared, 2019 appropriations remained incomplete. The 2019 column reflects at the account level enacted full-year appropriations provided for agencies funded in Public Law 115–244 and in divisions A and B of Public Law 115–245. For all other agencies, the 2019 column reflects annualized continuing appropriations provided under the Continuing Appropriations Act, 2019 (division C of Public Law 115–245, as amended). Any changes in mandatory programs (CHIMPs) enacted in full-year bills have been rebased as mandatory while any CHIMPs continuing under the 2019 continuing resolution are included in the 2019 column. The 2019 levels are further adjusted to illustratively reflect an alternative level in 2019 for the 2020 Decennial Census. An allowance is also included to reflect the current law caps for 2019 for defense and NDD.

[2] Funding for Food for Peace Title II Grants is included in the State and Other International Programs total. Although the funds are appropriated to the Department of Agriculture, the funds are administered by the U.S. Agency for International Development (USAID).

[3] The Department of Defense funding level in this presentation includes $9.2 billion requested as an emergency requirement to address border security and hurricane recovery.

[4] Funding from the Hospital Insurance and Supplementary Medical Insurance trust funds for administrative expenses incurred by the SSA that support the Medicare program are included in the HHS total and not in the SSA total.

[5] The total for HHS includes amounts authorized under the 21st Century Cures Act, which permitted funds to be appropriated each year for certain activities and not counted toward the discretionary caps so long as the appropriations were specifically provided for the authorized purposes.

[6] The State and International Programs total includes funding for the Department of State, USAID, Treasury International, and 12 international agencies.

[7] The total for the Department of the Treasury includes $0.4 billion for a new cap adjustment related to program integrity in the Internal Revenue Service. See the Budget Process chapter of the *Analytical Perspectives* volume of the Budget for more information on this adjustment.

[8] "Disaster Relief" appropriations are amounts designated as such by the Congress provided they are for activities carried out pursuant to a Presidential disaster declaration under the Robert T. Stafford Disaster Relief and Emergency Assistance Act. These amounts are held to a funding ceiling that is determined annually according to a statutory formula. Based on its 2020 Budget assumptions, OMB estimates the 2020 ceiling to be more than $21 billion and the Administration is requesting more than $19 billion for Disaster Relief in 2020 to address significant and unprecedented recovery needs of recent hurricanes and wildfires. The Budget does not explicitly request disaster-designated appropriations in any year after 2020 and a placeholder set at the 10-year average level is included in each of the outyears. The Administration's disaster relief request is discussed in greater detail in the Budget Process chapter of the *Analytical Perspectives* volume of the Budget.

[9] The 2020 Budget proposes to eliminate the Title 17 Innovative Technology Loan Guarantee Program and the Advanced Technology Vehicles Manufacturing Loan Program in the Department of Energy. This proposal includes a permanent cancellation of most of the remaining balances of emergency funding that were not designated pursuant to BBEDCA. This total also includes some smaller emergency cancellations in HUD. These cancellations are not being re-designated as emergency, therefore no savings are being achieved under the caps nor will the caps be adjusted for these cancellations.

Table S–9. Economic Assumptions[1]

(Calendar years)

	Actual	Projections											
	2017	2018	2019	2020	2021	2022	2023	2024	2025	2026	2027	2028	2029
Gross Domestic Product (GDP):													
Nominal level, billions of dollars	19,485	20,497	21,565	22,694	23,851	25,061	26,330	27,665	29,050	30,475	31,957	33,512	35,141
Percent change, nominal GDP, year/year	4.2	5.2	5.2	5.2	5.1	5.1	5.1	5.1	5.0	4.9	4.9	4.9	4.9
Real GDP, percent change, year/year	2.2	2.9	3.2	3.1	3.0	3.0	3.0	3.0	2.9	2.8	2.8	2.8	2.8
Real GDP, percent change, Q4/Q4	2.5	3.1	3.2	3.1	3.0	3.0	3.0	3.0	2.9	2.8	2.8	2.8	2.8
GDP chained price index, percent change, year/year	1.9	2.2	2.0	2.0	2.0	2.0	2.0	2.0	2.0	2.0	2.0	2.0	2.0
Consumer Price Index,[2] percent change, year/year	2.1	2.5	2.1	2.3	2.3	2.3	2.3	2.3	2.3	2.3	2.3	2.3	2.3
Interest rates, percent:[3]													
91-day Treasury bills[4]	0.9	1.9	2.7	3.1	3.2	3.2	3.1	3.0	3.0	3.0	3.0	3.0	3.0
10-year Treasury notes	2.3	2.9	3.4	3.6	3.8	3.8	3.7	3.7	3.7	3.7	3.7	3.7	3.7
Unemployment rate, civilian, percent[3]	4.4	3.9	3.6	3.6	3.7	3.9	4.0	4.1	4.2	4.2	4.2	4.2	4.2

Note: A more detailed table of economic assumptions appears in Chapter 2, "Economic Assumptions and Overview," in the *Analytical Perspectives* volume of the Budget.

[1] Based on information available as of mid-November 2018.

[2] Seasonally adjusted Consumer Price Index for all urban consumers.

[3] Annual average.

[4] Average rate, secondary market (bank discount basis).

Table S–10. Federal Government Financing and Debt

(Dollar amounts in billions)

	Actual 2018	Estimate 2019	2020	2021	2022	2023	2024	2025	2026	2027	2028	2029
Financing:												
Unified budget deficit:												
Primary deficit/surplus (–)	454	698	622	521	439	245	–1	–102	–185	–274	–301	–621
Net interest	325	393	479	548	610	664	702	733	762	788	810	823
Unified budget deficit	779	1,092	1,101	1,068	1,049	909	700	631	577	513	508	202
As a percent of GDP	3.9%	5.1%	4.9%	4.5%	4.2%	3.5%	2.6%	2.2%	1.9%	1.6%	1.5%	0.6%
Other transactions affecting borrowing from the public:												
Changes in financial assets and liabilities:[1]												
Change in Treasury operating cash balance	225	*	....	....	....	....	....	....	....	....	....	....
Net disbursements of credit financing accounts:												
Direct loan and Troubled Asset Relief Program (TARP) equity purchase accounts	91	48	67	68	66	65	65	65	61	58	58	52
Guaranteed loan accounts	–9	31	2	*	–2	–3	–4	–3	–3	–3	–3	–3
Net purchases of non-Federal securities by the National Railroad Retirement Investment Trust (NRRIT)	*	–1	–1	–1	–1	–1	–1	–1	–1	–*	–*	–*
Net change in other financial assets and liabilities[2]	–2	....	....	....	....	....	....	....	....	....	....	....
Subtotal, changes in financial assets and liabilities	305	78	68	67	63	61	60	61	57	54	54	49
Seigniorage on coins	–*	–*	–*	–*	–*	–*	–*	–*	–*	–*	–*	–*
Total, other transactions affecting borrowing from the public	305	77	67	67	63	61	60	61	57	54	54	48
Total, requirement to borrow from the public (equals change in debt held by the public)	1,084	1,169	1,168	1,135	1,112	970	760	692	634	567	562	251
Changes in Debt Subject to Statutory Limitation:												
Change in debt held by the public	1,084	1,169	1,168	1,135	1,112	970	760	692	634	567	562	251
Change in debt held by Government accounts	172	144	114	140	99	131	176	113	108	–*	–62	60
Change in other factors	10	2	3	2	2	2	2	2	2	2	2	2
Total, change in debt subject to statutory limitation	1,266	1,316	1,285	1,278	1,213	1,103	939	806	744	570	503	312
Debt Subject to Statutory Limitation, End of Year:												
Debt issued by Treasury	21,438	22,752	24,035	25,312	26,524	27,625	28,564	29,370	30,113	30,682	31,183	31,495
Adjustment for discount, premium, and coverage[3]	37	39	40	41	42	44	45	45	45	46	47	47
Total, debt subject to statutory limitation[4]	21,475	22,790	24,075	25,353	26,566	27,669	28,608	29,414	30,158	30,727	31,230	31,543
Debt Outstanding, End of Year:												
Gross Federal debt:[5]												
Debt issued by Treasury	21,438	22,752	24,035	25,312	26,524	27,625	28,564	29,370	30,113	30,682	31,183	31,495
Debt issued by other agencies	24	24	22	21	20	19	18	16	15	13	12	11
Total, gross Federal debt	21,462	22,776	24,057	25,333	26,544	27,645	28,582	29,386	30,128	30,695	31,195	31,506
As a percent of GDP	106.1%	107.0%	107.4%	107.5%	107.2%	106.3%	104.6%	102.4%	100.0%	97.2%	94.2%	90.7%

Table S–10. Federal Government Financing and Debt—Continued

(Dollar amounts in billions)

	Actual	Estimate										
	2018	2019	2020	2021	2022	2023	2024	2025	2026	2027	2028	2029
Held by:												
Debt held by Government accounts	5,713	5,857	5,971	6,111	6,210	6,341	6,517	6,630	6,738	6,738	6,676	6,736
Debt held by the public[6]	15,750	16,919	18,087	19,222	20,334	21,304	22,064	22,756	23,390	23,957	24,519	24,770
As a percent of GDP	77.8%	79.5%	80.7%	81.6%	82.1%	81.9%	80.7%	79.3%	77.7%	75.9%	74.0%	71.3%
Debt Held by the Public Net of Financial Assets:												
Debt held by the public	15,750	16,919	18,087	19,222	20,334	21,304	22,064	22,756	23,390	23,957	24,519	24,770
Less financial assets net of liabilities:												
Treasury operating cash balance	385	385	385	385	385	385	385	385	385	385	385	385
Credit financing account balances:												
Direct loan and TARP equity purchase accounts	1,372	1,420	1,486	1,554	1,620	1,686	1,750	1,815	1,877	1,934	1,992	2,044
Guaranteed loan accounts	5	36	37	37	36	32	29	25	22	19	16	13
Government-sponsored enterprise preferred stock	113	113	113	113	113	113	113	113	113	113	113	113
Non-Federal securities held by NRRIT	26	25	24	23	22	21	21	20	20	19	19	19
Other assets net of liabilities	–60	–60	–60	–60	–60	–60	–60	–60	–60	–60	–60	–60
Total, financial assets net of liabilities	1,840	1,918	1,986	2,053	2,116	2,178	2,238	2,299	2,356	2,411	2,465	2,514
Debt held by the public net of financial assets	13,910	15,001	16,101	17,169	18,218	19,126	19,826	20,457	21,033	21,546	22,054	22,256
As a percent of GDP	68.7%	70.5%	71.8%	72.9%	73.6%	73.5%	72.6%	71.3%	69.8%	68.2%	66.6%	64.1%

* $500 million or less.

[1] A decrease in the Treasury operating cash balance (which is an asset) is a means of financing a deficit and therefore has a negative sign. An increase in checks outstanding (which is a liability) is also a means of financing a deficit and therefore also has a negative sign.

[2] Includes checks outstanding, accrued interest payable on Treasury debt, uninvested deposit fund balances, allocations of special drawing rights, and other liability accounts; and, as an offset, cash and monetary assets (other than the Treasury operating cash balance), other asset accounts, and profit on sale of gold.

[3] Consists mainly of debt issued by the Federal Financing Bank (which is not subject to limit), the unamortized discount (less premium) on public issues of Treasury notes and bonds (other than zero-coupon bonds), and the unrealized discount on Government account series securities.

[4] Legislation enacted February 9, 2018 (Public Law 115–123), temporarily suspended the debt limit through March 1, 2019.

[5] Treasury securities held by the public and zero-coupon bonds held by Government accounts are almost all measured at sales price plus amortized discount or less amortized premium. Agency debt securities are almost all measured at face value. Treasury securities in the Government account series are otherwise measured at face value less unrealized discount (if any).

[6] At the end of 2018, the Federal Reserve Banks held $2,313.2 billion of Federal securities and the rest of the public held $13,436.4 billion. Debt held by the Federal Reserve Banks is not estimated for future years.

OMB CONTRIBUTORS TO THE 2020 BUDGET

The following personnel contributed to the preparation of this publication. Hundreds, perhaps thousands, of others throughout the Government also deserve credit for their valuable contributions.

A

Lindsay Abate
Andrew Abrams
Chandana L. Achanta
Brenda Aguilar
Shagufta Ahmed
P. Joseph Ahn
Steve Aitken
Lina Al Sudani
Joseph Albanese
Jason Alleman
Victoria Allred
Lois E. Altoft
Vishal Amin
Jessica A. Andreasen
Rachel Arguello
Anna R. Arroyo
Emily Schultz Askew
Lisa L. August
Renee Austin
Kristin B. Aveille

B

Jessie W. Bailey
Ally P. Bain
Coalter Baker
Paul W. Baker
Michelle Balch
Carol A. Bales
Pratik S. Banjade
Avital Bar-Shalom
Jody M. Barringer
Andrew Beehler
Jennifer Wagner Bell
Nathaniel Benjamin
Joseph J. Berger
Scott Bernard
Elizabeth A. Bernhard
William Bestani
Madison Biedermann
Mark Bigley
Emily R. Bilbao
Bradley Bishop
Samuel J. Black
Robert B. Blair
Mathew C. Blum
Fernandez Boards
James Boden
Sharon A. Boivin
Amira C. Boland
Cassie L. Boles
Melissa B. Bomberger
David Bottom
William J. Boyd
Mollie Bradlee
Sean W. T. Branchaw
Michael Branson
Alex M. Brant
Joseph F. Breighner
Julie A. Brewer
Andrea M. Brian
Candice M. Bronack
Katie Broomell
Dustin S. Brown
Sheila Bruce
Michael T. Brunetto
Pearl Buenvenida
Tom D. Bullers
Scott H. Burgess
Ben Burnett
Jordan C. Burris
Meghan K. Burris
John C. Burton
Nicholas S. Burton
Mark Bussow
Sean Butler
Dylan W. Byrd

C

Steve E. Cahill
Alexandra Campana
Anthony Campau
Amy Canfield
Benjamin B. Cantrell
Eric Cardoza
Kevin Carpenter
Curtis M. Carr
Kerrie Carr
William S. S. Carroll
Scott D. Carson
Sean C. Casey
Mary I. Cassell
James Chase
Nida Chaudhary
Michael Chelen
Anita Chellaraj
Peter Choi
Gezime Christian
Michael Clark
Gregory A. Clayton
Angela Colamaria
William P. Cole
Victoria W. Collin
Debra M. Collins
Kelly T. Colyar
Ann Conant
Jose A. Conde
Alyson M. Conley
David Connolly
Jeannette Mandycz Connor
Matthew Conway
Aaron Cooke
LaTiesha B. Cooper
Matthew T. Cornelius
Drew W. Cramer
Catherine E. Crato
William Creedon
Tyler Overstreet Cromer
Rose Crow
James Crowe
Juliana Crump
Craig Crutchfield
David M. Cruz-Glaudemans
Lily Cuk
Pennee Cumberlander
Laura Cunliffe
C. Tyler Curtis
William Curtis
Charles R. Cutshall
Matthew Cutts

D

Nadir Dalal
D. Michael Daly
Rody Damis
Neil B. Danberg
Elisabeth C. Daniel
Charlie Dankert
Quadira R. Dantro
Kristy L. Daphnis
Alexander J. Daumit
Joanne Chow Davenport
Kenneth L. Davis
Margaret B. Davis-Christian
Chad J. Day
Brandon F. DeBruhl
Tasha M. Demps
Paul J. Denaro
Laura Dennehy
Catherine A. Derbes
Antonio Diaz-Agosto
John H. Dick
Amie Didlo
Kerry Wisdom Dittmeier
Angela M. Donatelli
Paul S. Donohue
Vladik Dorjets
Michelle Dorsey
Anjelica B. Dortch
Emma Doyle
Megan Dreher
Lisa Cash Driskill
Mark A. Dronfield

Whitney Duffey-Jones
John Dugan
Carolyn R. Dula-Wilson

E

Matthew C. Eanes
Jacqueline A. Easley
Calie Edmonds
Jeanette Edwards
Tonya L. Ellison-Mays
Michelle Enger
Diana F. Epstein
Edward V. Etzkorn
Patrick Evans

F

Farnoosh Faezi-Marian
Robert Fairweather
Ladan Fakory
Edna Falk Curtin
Hunter Fang
Kara L. Farley-Cahill
Christine E. Farquharson
Emily R. Feagans
Christopher M. Felix
Lesley A. Field
Leah R. Fine
Jonathan K. Finer
Sean Finnegan
Mary S. Fischietto
Brette Fishman
John J. Fitzpatrick
Daniel G. Fowlkes
Nicholas A. Fraser
Haley Friedman
Jake Fuller

G

Scott D. Gaines
James Galkowski
Janice D. Gallant
Christopher D. Gamache
Mar Gamboa
Joseph R. Ganahl
Kyle Gardiner
Mathias A. Gardner
Marisol Garibay
Marc Garufi
Thomas O. Gates
Daniel Giamo
Paul A. Gill
Brian Gillis
Janelle R. Gingold
Nicoletta S. Giordani
Jacob Glass
Joshua S. Glazer
Andrea L. Goel
Jeffrey D. Goldstein
Anthony A. Gonzalez
Oscar Gonzalez
Alex Goodenough
Margie Graves
John W. Gray
Aron Greenberg
Brandon H. Greene
Justin Grimes
Gina K. Grippando
Hester C. Grippando
Joe Grogan
Andrea L. Grossman
Kerry Gutknecht

H

Michael B. Hagan
Tia Hall
Tamara S. Hamaty
William F. Hamele
Amy Hamilton
Daniel Hanlon
Brian Hanson
Jennifer L. Hanson
David T. Hardin
Linda W. Hardin
Dionne Hardy
Robert Harkinson
Deidre A. Harrison
Edward Hartwig
Paul Harvey
Kyle Hathaway
Laurel Havas
Nichole M. Hayden
Mark Hazelgren
John David Henson
Kevin W. Herms
Rachel Hernández
Jim Herz
David Hester
Alexander G. Hettinger
Gretchen T. Hickey
Michael J. Hickey
Amanda M. Hill
Jonathan Hill
Elaine P. Ho
Elke Hodson-Marten
Jennifer E. Hoef
Jason Hoffman
Stuart Hoffman
Troy Holland
Michele Holt
Lynette Hornung
Jack Hoskins
Grace Hu
Jamie W. Huang
Rhea A. Hubbard
Kathy M. Hudgins
Jay Huie
Shristi Humagai
Sally J. Hunnicutt
Alexander T. Hunt
Lorraine D. Hunt
William Hunt
James C. Hurban
Veta Hurst
Nathan Hurwitz

I

Tae H. Im
Mason C. Ingram
Elizabeth R. Irwin

J

Manish Jain
Varun M. Jain
Harrison M. Jarrett
Bryan E. Jefferson
Carol Jenkins
Carol Johnson
Michael D. Johnson
Danielle Y. Jones
Denise Bray Jones
Lisa M. Jones
Othni A. Jones
Colby Ryan Jordan
Hee Jun

K

Paul A. Kagan
Daniel S. Kaneshiro
Jacob H. Kaplan
Regina L. Kearney
Matthew J. Keeneth
Hunter S. Kellett
Nancy B. Kenly
Suzette Kent
Meshach E. Keye
Saha Khaterzai
Shubha Khot
Jordan T. Kiesel
Paul E. Kilbride
Jung H. Kim
Rachael Y. Kim
Barry King
Kelly C. King
Kelly A. Kinneen
David E. Kirkpatrick
Benjamin W. Klay
Robert T. Klein
April Kluever
James O. Knable
Andrea G. Korovesis
Katelyn V. Koschewa
Faride Kraft
Lori A. Krauss
Steven B. Kuennen
Jennifer J. Kuk
Yaropolk T. Kulchyckyj
Christine Kymn

L

Christopher D. LaBaw
Erik LaDue
Jon W. Ladyga
Leonard L. Lainhart
James A. Laity
Chad A. Lallemand
Lawrence L. Lambert
Michael Landry
Kelley C. Lane
Daniel LaPlaca
Anthony Larkins
Derek B. Larson
Connie LaSalle
Ashley P. Lau
Eric P. Lauer
Jessie L. LaVine
Suzette Lawson
Christopher Leach
Jessica Lee
Susan E. Leetmaa
Annika N. Lescott
Kerrie Leslie
Malissa C. Levesque
John C. Levock-Spindle

Bryan León
Sheila Lewis
Wendy L. Liberante
Richard Alan Lichtenberger
Kristina E. Lilac
Erika Liliedahl
John E. Lindner
Adam Lipton
Kimberly Lopez
Sara R. López
Adrienne Lucas
Gideon F. Lukens

M

Patrick D. Macatangga
Deborah Macaulay
Ryan MacMaster
Claire A. Mahoney
Dominic J. Mancini
Noah S. Mann
Sharon Mar
Brendan A. Martin
Rochelle Martinez
James Massot
Nicholas T. Matich IV
Kimie Matsuo
Salim Mawani
Shelly McAllister
Jessica Rae McBean
Alexander J. McClelland
Malcolm McConnell
Jeremy P. McCrary
Connor G. McCrone
Jennifer McDannell
Anthony W. McDonald
Cheryl McDonald
Christine A. McDonald
Katrina A. McDonald
Renford McDonald
Kevin E. McGinnis
Kyle L. McIntyre
Natalie McIntyre
Charlie E. McKiver
Moutray McLaren
Michael McManus
William McNavage
Melissa R. Medeiros
Inna L. Melamed
Barbara A. Menard
Flavio Menasce
P. Thaddeus Messenger
William L. Metzger
Daniel J. Michelson-Horowitz
Julie L. Miller
Kimberly Miller
Susan M. Minson
Mia Mitchell
Emily A. Mok
Kirsten J. Moncada
Claire Monteiro
Joseph Montoni
Caroline Moore
Kelly Morrison
William Morrison
Morgan Mosack
Robin McLaughry Mullins
Mick Mulvaney
Jonathan Murphy
Christian G. Music
Hayley W. Myers
Kimberley L Myers

N

Jennifer Nading
Jeptha E. Nafziger
Larry J. Nagl
Barry Napear
Robert Nassif
Kimberly P. Nelson
Melissa K. Neuman
Joanie F. Newhart
Kimberly Armstrong Newman
Anthony (Tony) Nguyen
Teresa O. Nguyen
Tim H. Nusraty
Frederick Nutt
Joseph B. Nye

O

Erin O'Brien
Matthew J. O'Kane
Brendan J. O'Meara
Matthew Oreska
Frederick H. Orndorff
Noah J. Osman
Jared Ostermiller

P

Benjamin J. Page
Heather C. Pajak
Rosario Palmieri
Mark R. Paoletta
Farrah Pappa
Peggy A. Parker
John C. Pasquantino
Jagir Patel
Neal A. Patel
Mary Beth E. Pavlik
Brian Paxton
Terri Payne
Liuyi Pei
Falisa L. Peoples-Tittle
Michael A. Perz
Whitney L. Peters
Andrea M. Petro
Alexandra Petrucci
Amy E. Petz
Stacey Que-Chi Pham
Carolyn R. Phelps
Karen A. Pica
Brian Pipa
Joseph Pipan
Adrian Plater
Ruxandra Pond
Julianne Poston
Nancy Potok
Larrimer S. Prestosa
Jamie M. Price
Alanna Pugliese
Robert B. Purdy

R

Lucas R. Radzinschi
Latonda Glass Raft
Moshiur Rahman
Aaron D. Ray
James M. Read
Alex Reed
Rudolph G. Regner
Paul B. Rehmus
Thomas M. Reilly
Bryant D. Renaud
Keri A. Rice
Shannon A. Richter
Natalie Rico
Kyle S. Riggs
Emma K. Roach
Beth Higa Roberts
Taylor C. Roberts
Donovan Robinson
Marshall J. Rodgers
Christina Rodriguez
Colin Rom
Meredith B. Romley
Jeffrey R. Ross
Sean Rough
David J. Rowe
Mario D. Roy
Danielle Royal
Jacqueline Rudas
Erika H. Ryan

S

Fouad P. Saad
John Asa Saldivar
Alvand A. Salehi
Dannia Salem
Mark S. Sandy
Ruth Saunders
Joel Savary
Jeff Schlagenhauf
Grant Schneider
Daniel K. Schory
Nancy E. Schwartz
Mariarosaria Sciannameo
Jasmeet K. Seehra
Kimberly Segura
Robert B. Seidner
Andrew Self
Megan Shade
Shahid N. Shah
Shabnam Sharbatoghlie
Amy K. Sharp
Dianne Shaughnessy
Paul Shawcross
David Shorkrai
Gary F. Shortencarrier
Letticia Sierra
Sara R. Sills
Daniel Liam Singer
Robert Sivinski
Benjamin J. Skidmore
Richard A. Skokowski
Jonathan Slemrod
Curtina O. Smith
Somer Smith
Stannis M. Smith
Rachel B. Snyderman
Silvana Solano
Roderic A. Solomon

Timothy F. Soltis
Amanda R.K. Sousane
Rebecca L. Spavins
Raquel A. Spencer
Valeria Spinner
Sarah Whittle Spooner
Travis C. Stalcup
Scott R. Stambaugh
Nora Stein
Lamar R. Stewart
Ryan Stoffers
Gary R. Stofko
Terry W. Stratton
Thomas J. Suarez
Alec J. Sugarman
Kevin J. Sullivan
Jessica L. Sun
Yasaman S. Sutton
Christina Swoope
Katherine M. Sydor

T

Jamie R. Taber
John Tambornino
Naomi S. Taransky
Jay Teitelbaum
Emma K. Tessier
Matthew A. Tetteh
Rich Theroux
Amanda L. Thomas
Payton A. Thomas
Will Thomas
Philip Tizzani
Thomas Tobasko
Gia Tonic
Gil M. Tran
Alyssa Trinidad
Kim Marie V. Tuminaro
Austin Turner

U

Nicholas J. Ufier
Shraddha A. Upadhyaya
Darrell J. Upshaw
Taylor J. Urbanski
Euler V. Uy

V

Matthew J. Vaeth
Cynthia Vallina
Sarita Vanka
Areletha L. Venson
Alexandra Ventura
Russ Vought

W

Dana Wade
James A. Wade
Brett Waite
Nicole Waldeck
Heather V. Walsh
Kan Wang
Tim Wang
Peter Warren
Gary Waxman
Bess M. Weaver
Jacqueline K. Webb
Margaret Weichert
Jeffrey A. Weinberg
David Weisshaar
Philip R. Wenger
Max W. West
Steve Wetzel
Arnette C. White
Ashley M. White
Catherine E. White
Curtis C. White
Kim S. White
Sherron R. White
Chad S. Whiteman
Brian Widuch
Mary Ellen Wiggins
Rayna Wilkins
Debra (Debbie) L. Williams
Michael B. Williams
Rebecca Williams
Ken D. Willis
Jamie S. Wilson
Paul A. Winters
Minzy Won
Raymond J.M. Wong
Jacob Wood
Rachel P. Wood
Sophia M. Wright
Bert Wyman

Y

Jason Yaworske
Melany N. Yeung
Sin Yeung
David Y. Yi
Katey Yoast
Rita Young
Robert A. Yu

Z

Eliana M. Zavala
Jen Q. Zhu
Erica H. Zielewski